Why Christianity makes sense

John Pritchard

First published in Great Britain in 2014

Society for Promoting Christian Knowledge
36 Causton Street
London SW1P 4ST
www.spckpublishing.co.uk

British Library Cataloguing-in-Publication Data
A catalogue record for this book is available from the British Library

ISBN 978–0–281–06764–0
eBook ISBN 978–0–281–06765–7

Typeset by Graphicraft Limited, Hong Kong
First printed in Great Britain by Ashford Colour Press

eBook by Graphicraft Limited, Hong Kong

Produced on paper from sustainable forests

Contents

A word at the beginning

I was wondering what I'd learned from a week in the ecumenical French community of Taizé. It had been a very refreshing week and I was writing out my thoughts in a journal as I often do. I found myself asking, 'What do I really believe about God? And what do I really not believe about God?' Let's have ten points to keep it crisp. And while we're on the subject, why do people have problems about faith, and why does Christianity *work*? The idea developed before I left Taizé: Ten Commandments for today, ten ways of praying, ten values for tomorrow's Church, and so on.

Why the figure ten? For two reasons: first, people seem to be fascinated with lists, and second, we love statistics. Newspapers print lists of the ten bestselling books or CDs/downloads. They tell us the 100 richest people in Britain or the five best-performing investment companies. My history magazine last month had the ten most significant battles (surely an impossible task) and eight places to meet the Tudor navy. I have a whole book full of lists, many of which are almost certainly of no possible interest to any reasonable person. It seems we can't get enough of lists.

At the same time, statistics seem to keep us completely fascinated. Try these:

- 250 – the number of miles a migrating red admiral butterfly can travel in a day.
- 70 – the percentage of National Lottery millionaires who don't employ a cleaner.
- 400 – the number of people in the USA who together own half the country's assets.
- 20 – the average number of minutes a power drill in Britain is used in its entire life.

- 55 – the percentage of the world's pigs that live in China.
- 22 – the number of countries (out of nearly 200) that have never experienced a British invasion.

(I bet you wanted to know all that . . .)

So I thought I would take the number ten and make lists around that significant number. It's a gimmick really, but it allows me to reflect on many years of ministry and offer a kind of distillation of where I've got to about what really matters. I hope it's the kind of book that encourages Christians to recognize the contours of their own faith, and also one they can put into the hands of friends and say, 'See if that kind of faith makes sense.' I've tried to be clear, but to keep away from dogmatism. I hope to have represented a generous orthodoxy for the mind and a gracious spirituality for the heart.

The famous Methodist minister Leslie Weatherhead once said that the gospel is something that can be shouted across the street, like: 'The baby's arrived!' or 'Simon's out of danger!' What are the things that we would shout? This book is my attempt to say some of them.

One point that might be worth noting is that the chapters don't have to be read in the order they appear. Some chapters are linked to others but each list has its own integrity. You might choose to read them simply as they interest you. At the end of each section I've included a brief set of questions for groups: I think there's plenty of scope for people to improve on my lists.

I've written this book on sabbatical and am very grateful to those who worked extra hard to cover my absence: Bishop Colin Fletcher, my chaplain Amanda Bloor, PA Christine Lodge and secretary Debbie Perry. My editor Alison Barr faithfully oversaw the project, as she has many others, and trustingly left me to it for most of the time. I dedicate this book, gratefully, to her.

John Pritchard

1

Ten problems people have with faith

Only ten? Well, I've grouped them. They're familiar territory to most of us, not only because of the hissing secular static that has become the background noise of our culture, but also because we've probably faced some of these questions ourselves. The black crow of doubt is quite likely to flap across our minds from time to time, and engaging with that big bird should bring us to a firmer, and perhaps more realistic, faith. People are now much more prepared to be outspoken about what they don't believe and Christians don't need to look hurt and run for cover, or to muddle through on a whinge and a prayer, but to rise happily to the challenge of presenting a cogent and attractive reason for the hope that is in us.

1 Faith is a fairy tale

Some think that faith is believing when there's no evidence, a story made up by earlier civilizations to answer their big questions by projecting a comfort blanket into the heavens. In fact, they say, there is as little evidence of God as there is of Bertrand Russell's celestial teapot orbiting the earth. We should let primitive beliefs go, or at least treat them in the same way as Father Christmas, a comforting story with seasonal value.

There is, of course, no way of proving the existence of God because God is not an object to put under a microscope or observe through a telescope, but the question of evidence is important. What should count as evidence? Surely not only what can be weighed and measured. Can we buy a kilo of courage or measure out three metres of compassion? Is a great symphony true? Is mercy something you prove in an equation? Is a kiss just the coming together of two pairs of lips for the mutual transmission of microbes and carbon dioxide? Evidence is not the sole prerogative of science; it belongs also to philosophy, poetry, art, theology and human relationships.

Moreover, if all civilizations have always had some form of sacred canopy in their belief system, perhaps there really is a transcendent reality that corresponds to that belief; it doesn't automatically have to be a human construct. While Freud believed that religious faith was the comforting illusion that there is a cosmic father figure out there, it could equally be argued that atheism is the comforting illusion that there is *no* father figure and you can get away with doing anything you feel like. Indeed, living your life without a religious framework can be positively dangerous. Rabbi Jonathan Sacks said in a lecture: 'A society without faith is like one without art, music, beauty or grace, and no society without faith can endure for long.'[1]

2 Religion is out of date, out of time and out of supporters

In the 1960s, 70s and 80s the worldly wise were confidently predicting the end of the religious era and the victory of secularism. Such a claim looks somewhat extravagant and ill-informed today. Take China, where the rate of growth of the Church suggests that by 2050 it will have the largest number of Christians in the world (and the largest number of Muslims); meanwhile 99 per cent of Indonesians and 98 per cent of Egyptians say that religion plays an important part in their lives. It's commonly understood by politicians that religion is a major factor in geopolitical issues; no political think-tank or elite military academy will ignore it. From wealthy mega-churches in the United States to mosques packed with young men in the Middle East, from resurgent Buddhism in the Far East to black and Asian churches in east London, religion is driving forward in numbers and influence. Sometimes, of course, a particular expression of religion becomes unhealthy, as happens to all basic human instincts (hunger, sex, pride, ambition). But the one thing that cannot be said is that religion is on its way out. Indeed, in the daily scramble to survive amidst the glittering wreckage of our sex and celebrity culture, it could be said that strong, healthy religion is becoming a necessity. Society's over-the-counter prescriptions aren't enough to deal with deep-seated issues of meaning, identity and values. You can't rely on popcorn to fix malnutrition. The smart money is no longer on secularism.

3 God is a despot

This is the extreme version of the problems people have with belief in God. Consider this modest evaluation from Richard Dawkins:

> The God of the Old Testament is arguably the most unpleasant character in all fiction: jealous and proud of it; a petty, unjust, unforgiving control-freak; a vindictive, bloodthirsty ethnic cleanser; a misogynistic, homophobic, racist, infanticidal, genocidal, filicidal, pestilential, megalomaniacal, sadomasochistic, capriciously malevolent bully.[2]

Such a god would indeed be appalling. Sadly, Dawkins is not reading the Bible with the sophistication he would expect of someone reading scientific texts.

The Bible is not only God's book about humanity; it's humanity's book about God, and as such is the record of an evolving understanding of the mystery we can never contain or describe. Falteringly, the writers came to fuller, richer understandings of God, but from the start they had seen that this was a love story about a Creator with a fierce and faithful longing for his people, and whose love was absolute. 'When Israel was a child,

I loved him' (Hos. 11.1). 'When you pass through the waters, I will be with you; and through the rivers, they shall not over-whelm you . . . You are precious in my sight, and honoured, and I love you' (Isa. 43.4). The Bible shows us in epic form how God's people understood their destiny and their special relationship with the protector they knew as Yahweh. And ultimately we see the fulfilment of God's loving purpose for all humanity in the life, death and new life of Jesus of Nazareth. It's an amazing story, and not helped by being read as if it's a Harry Potter novel.

4 Faith is incompatible with science

I want to explore this in Chapter 6, but it's clearly an issue that colours the water across our whole culture. Here is philosopher Julian Baggini: 'It is not true that science challenges only the most primitive, literal forms of religion. It is probably going too far to say that science makes the God of Christianity, Judaism and Islam impossible, but it certainly makes him very unlikely indeed.'[3] On the other hand, Professor John Polking-horne believes that in the scientific community there are prob-ably more convinced Christians than convinced atheists.[4] Many scientists who are Christians find that the discoveries of cosmology and quantum physics make God both larger and more amazing than ever. Certainly, the half-gods must go: the small, tribal view of a God who looks after me and my friends, and loses his way outside my little world of self-interest. But our understanding of the glorious God whose narrative describes an arc of breathtaking beauty from Genesis to Revelation is vastly enhanced when scientists bring back their findings from the far reaches of their research. The Nobel prize-winning physicist Max Planck said: 'Anyone who has seriously engaged in scientific work of any kind realizes that over the entrance to the gate of the temple of science are written the words, "You must have faith".'[5] Einstein's famous aphorism was:

'Science without religion is lame, religion without science is blind.'[6]

Scientists and theologians are fellow researchers engaged with the one reality. They encounter this reality from different directions but only together do they make the fullest sense of the astonishing world that has been given to us. A painting can be described in terms of the chemical nature of its pigments or as the *Mona Lisa*. Music is a sequence of vibrations experienced in the inner ear or it's Beethoven's Ninth Symphony. Sexual feelings can be described in terms of various genetic strategies or in terms of devotion, fidelity, betrayal, and so on. We mustn't live down to our lowest descriptions of reality but live up to the highest descriptions of which humanity is capable. Science and religion do that best together, combining the facts and figures with the poetry.

5 Faith has no answer to evil and suffering

Does anyone? Even if the problem of evil is no more difficult than the problem of good, who would dare to offer explanations by the bedside of a dying child? Everything in us should protest at such an outrage. Suffering isn't an algebraic problem to solve; it's an agony to be borne as well as we can. But if we're forced to say anything in this dark arena it can at least be argued that a world developing through evolutionary mutations and acting freely according to its nature is compatible with a God who loves us like any lover: that is, one who restricts his freedom so that we can have ours, and who never, ever leaves us. The processes of nature interact, sometimes constructively and sometimes destructively. If these processes were programmed so no collision was ever possible, our world would be a rigid set of independent phenomena, without the possibilities of creativity, love or courage. A world where God constantly stepped in with warnings and miracles would be no world where free agents could operate, let alone flourish.

This means that natural disasters are just that – the laws and regularities of nature getting on with their job. Tragically it also means that a child abuser can arise and do untold damage, or cancer strike down a young mother. Life on earth is a much riskier and more unpredictable experience than we might like, but at least it's got texture, at least it's *real*. There's no explanation for suffering, only participation. God participates in it fully, as we've seen in the way Jesus was flogged, beaten and scraped over a cross. He has travelled that dark road too. And still God pours his being into the world, bringing life and potentiality to every part and every person, especially when love and hope break down. He invites us to participate too, in love, in action, in silence, above all in attentive presence alongside those who walk that lonely road of wrecked dreams.

6 Faith is intolerant and often leads to violence

It's easy to see how this problem emerges. History demonstrates that people of religion can be very intolerant over matters about which they feel strongly. The normal list includes the Crusades, the so-called Wars of Religion, the Inquisition, the Irish question, Islamic jihadists and more. Christians, for their part, must put their hands up. But it wasn't the religion of Jesus Christ that they represented in their violence; it was the religion of men (mostly). The scrap yard of the human heart gives birth to all sorts of passions as we make our angry journeys to Damascus. The answer to this darkness is not to try to get rid of it (equals: getting rid of human beings); the answer is to pour in more light.

I want to quote at some length what David Bentley Hart says in his book *Atheist Delusions*:

> I maintain that to speak of the evil of religion or to desire its abolition is as simpleminded as condemning and wanting to abolish politics. Dennett, for example [Daniel Dennett, atheist

philosopher], on several occasions in *Breaking the Spell* proclaims his devotion to democracy, a devotion that one can assume remains largely undiminished by the knowledge that democratic governments – often in the name of protecting or promoting democracy – have waged unjust wars, incinerated villages or cities full of non-combatants, abridged civil liberties, tolerated corruption and racial inequality, lied to their citizens, aided despotic foreign regimes, or given power to evil men (Hitler seems a not insignificant example of this last) . . . What I find most mystifying in the arguments of the authors I have mentioned is the strange presupposition that a truly secular society would of its nature be more tolerant and less prone to violence than any society shaped by any form of faith. Given that the modern age of secular governance has been the most savagely and sublimely violent period in human history, by a factor (or body count) of incalculable magnitude, it is hard to identify the grounds for their confidence.[7]

Pouring in 'more light' means, for the Christian, not less faith but more of the just and peace-loving faith of Jesus Christ, which has proven time and again to be able to change people's hearts and behaviour.

7 Faith is life-denying and negative

The words of the poet Algernon Swinburne are echoed by many: 'Thou hast conquered, O pale Galilean; the world has grown grey from thy breath.'[8] It's a depressing view of the impact of Jesus Christ but one that Christians need to hear. There can be a depressing moralism about the way the Church appears to the uncommitted, and indeed there is such a condition as 'death by religion'. To put it bluntly, churches can sometimes be short of sunshine.

My own experience of faith starts from somewhere completely different. What first drew me to Christian commitment was the rich, colourful figure of Jesus, meandering through

Galilee with a group of friends and offering the most compelling vision of what human life is about. I then came across a verse in John's Gospel (10.10) which puts it perfectly. Jesus said: 'I have come that they may have life, and have it abundantly.' My experience of faith has been of life lived in full colour and HD. That doesn't mean we aren't battle-scarred or don't have bleak periods when life fades to black and white, but it does mean that the possibility I'm offered by faith is of a fullness and freshness far beyond my normal limits. The writer Marilynne Robinson (author of *Gilead* and *Home*) uses another image:

> I definitely went through a period when I thought I would make the experiment of unbelief, and it lasted several months, and it felt so wrong. It was as if the ceiling of the universe had come down, so that it was just over my head. By attempting not to think in religious terms, the validity of religious terms came rushing back, and from that point on I dreaded the idea of a contracted universe.[9]

That's a telling phrase: 'a contracted universe'. The Church will often fail us but the Christian faith it tries bravely to express gives access to a universe that expands to infinity.

8 Christianity is for failures

Then it's for me! All of us are a mixture of success and failure in different proportions at different times. One of the gifts of the nihilist Friedrich Nietzsche was to despise Christianity for what it actually was – a faith based on compassion for every single person, and corresponding care for the weak, the outcast and the infirm. He also had the honesty to recognize that you couldn't do away with Christian faith and retain a diluted form of Christian morality such as innate human sympathy or liberal social conscience. His 'Superman' creates his own universe and his will to power is the very essence of his existence. He has no time for the enfeebling ways of Christian *agape*-love.

But I have difficulties with the bluster of 'man-made' success. It rarely rings true. The pastor in me has met too much frailty in apparently successful people. And as someone said: nothing recedes like success.

I can't really trust a society that sees success in superficial codes like celebrity, wealth, good looks and a full diary. Success isn't saying yes to everything, because we then find we're satisfied by nothing. I see something approaching primal chaos in parts of our success-oriented culture as the drive for money distorts and divides our communities. I would much prefer to look to the 'ancient mariners' of the faith, the saints and thinkers of old, to find wisdom for the long haul. The success of a competitive, materialist culture is a poor benchmark. The same applies to the Church when we're seduced by the contemporary world's understanding of success. We don't remember who was running the mega-churches of the middle ages; instead we remember St Francis and his care of lepers. So I don't mind the charge that Christianity is for failures because that means it's for everyone. And that's what I find in our churches, where people of every background and income sit side by side, equally valued by God.

9 The Church is a regressive institution

You can understand where this critique gains traction. The insular navel-gazing that has gone on for years over gender (women bishops) and sexuality (gay relationships) has made the Church appear to belong to another age. Society has by and large gone past these issues, and struggles with other agendas such as national security, financial breakdown, climate change and global poverty. Why would people want to join what looks like a dysfunctional organization when they've got enough dysfunctionality of their own? The point this misses, however, is that the local church is one of the most fruitful and significant institutions in society, and these churches act as launch-pads for countless acts of grace. Charles Clarke, Home Secretary from 2004 to 2006, wrote in *The Tablet*:

> My work in inner-city Hackney in the early 1980s convinced me, despite my personal agnosticism, that the contribution of religion overall is usually a force for good. Almost every leader of the voluntary, community and charitable organisations which promoted education, social care and community strength, did it because of their own committed religious faith.[10]

Where does such care come from? In an editorial in *The Week*, Jeremy O'Grady wrote:

> One has only to examine the dire status of 'care for the elderly', 'community care' and 'children in care' to realise that secular society isn't very good at caring. In their assault on religion, god-slayers and ghost-busters like Richard Dawkins gloss this point. But if you need someone to care for the lonely, the sick, the brutalised, who are you going to call – Mother Teresa or Christopher Hitchens?[11]

(Both now sadly dead, of course.) Moreover, you can't have Christian ethics without Christian communities. The values are shaped in communities of particular character, and that character has 'faith' written right through it. On their day, churches are amazing.

10 All faiths are the same

This charge doesn't go down too well with people of any of the world's great faith traditions, and not because they think ill of one another's religion. It's simply that it's lazy thinking to suppose that all faiths are the same. Each is distinct, with its own set of beliefs and practices, deeply rooted in a centuries-old tradition, and respected for its own particular insights into human nature and the character of the divine. To conflate them all into a grey religious porridge does no credit to anyone. What is often actually being said is: 'All faiths are the same, so that lets me off having to engage with any of them.' It's an escape hatch from serious thinking. There are, of course, common threads and we can rejoice in the things that hold us together – the most fundamental of which is probably the call to live compassionately with other human beings and with the rest of nature. But the great faith traditions have an integrity of their own and it's from that uniqueness that dialogues of mutual respect can begin.

Story

The famous physicist Albert Einstein was once travelling on a train when the conductor came down the carriage to check the tickets. When he came to Einstein the great man couldn't find his ticket. He tried every pocket, his briefcase, the seat, the floor, but there was no sign of it. The conductor said, 'Dr Einstein, I know who you are. I'm sure you bought your ticket. Don't worry about it.' Then he moved on, but as he was about to enter the next carriage, he looked back and saw Einstein crawling about the floor on his hands and knees. He rushed back in dismay and said again, 'Please don't worry, Dr Einstein. It's not a problem. I know who you are.'

Einstein looked at him and said, 'Young man, like you, I know who I am. What I don't know is where I'm going.'

Do we?

Taking it further

These ten problems people have with faith may be ones you recognize or even share. There may be others you think are just as important. They can be the basis of a stimulating discussion. How would you answer the charges? What else would you say?

2

Ten things I believe about God

———— ◆•◆•◆ ————

1 God is not somewhere else

For many years I mounted regular search parties to find where God had gone into hiding. God wasn't answering the phone or turning up at the door as in the past, so I went looking. The cunning thing was that I was actually taking God with me even as I went looking; it's just that I hadn't noticed. If we look for God in spiritual fireworks of the New Year's Eve variety, we might not notice God in the modest spiritual sparklers that surround us all the time. God is not somewhere else. God can only be present to us at this moment, in this place, and nowhere else. God is always present if we are, the problem being that often we're the one who's not at home.

Once we become aware of the way the present moment is saturated with the presence of God, nothing much may change in the outer world but much may shift in our inner one. The street is more alive and colourful; a conversation becomes more interesting; a piece of work has more potential; love leaks in, quick as a smile. The dull plod of the spiritual search party is called off. There's a more energizing and immediate way to live with God. The writer G. K. Chesterton was once asked by a reporter: 'If the risen Christ suddenly appeared at this very moment and stood behind you, what would you do?' Chesterton looked the reporter straight in the eye and said: 'He is.'

2 God is inexhaustible

I used to struggle with the old conundrum that if God is all-powerful and all-loving then the terrible things that happen in this life shouldn't happen. So either God can't be all-powerful or God can't be all-loving. As I wanted to hang on to both characteristics this was a bit of a bother. Bishop John V. Taylor finally cracked it for me when he wrote this: 'The truth about God is not so much that he is omnipotent as that he is inexhaustible, and for that reason he will always succeed.'[1] Omnipotence is a somewhat iron-and-concrete concept; it has no fluidity or flexibility. But to be inexhaustible means that the resources God brings to every situation are limitless and that God never, ever gives up. Such relentless loving is ultimately irresistible – 'he will always succeed'. What that means in the world of here and now isn't predictable, but if God is God, his purposes of love must ultimately come through and all things be gathered up in him (Eph. 1.10).

The metaphor that works for me is of a mountain stream, a mere trickle to begin with, high up where the big birds fly free. As it tumbles down the mountainside the stream encounters a blockage of stones, branches and old foliage, but the stream isn't put off. It finds a way, not through the blockage, but over, under, or round the side. On it rushes, increasingly fed by other streams, until it runs into a bigger problem, a landslip giving significant resistance. But again the stream isn't deterred; it endlessly innovates and finds a way over, under, or round the side. On it goes, fuller, more confident now, encountering each obstacle with vitality and imagination, always finding a way, always getting through. Eventually it pours into the big river which rolls irresistibly to the sea; nothing can ultimately withstand its persuasive insistence. It's a good picture of the loving activity of God, patiently finding a way through all that opposes the ways of love, justice and peace. God is not 'omnipotent' as in the old ways of thinking, but inexhaustible.

Ultimately God could withdraw from creation and it would cease to be, but as long as he sustains this creation, it will be loved into submission.

3 God is always more

I do worry about what kind of God some people believe in. They seem to have a domestic, family-sized God in mind, an off-the-peg deity, not so loud as to frighten the neighbours, and not so radical as to upset their lifestyle. Such a God usually needs protection from the nasty people who are rude about him and call him names. Protect God? I'd rather protect a tiger or an earthquake or a storm on the sun. If God *is* at all, then he's the God of Everything, which means the 10 billion, trillion stars in the visible universe and all the molecules in a single glass of water, the number of which is greater than the number of glasses of water in all the world's oceans. The scale of the universe is simply staggering. The light from some stars has been heading our way at 186,000 miles per second since before Jesus was born. And that's just the start; some light has been coming at us at that speed for 13.7 billion years! That's quite some distance. And God is the God of all of that. This is no small-town deity struggling to keep a foothold in society or get a mention in the weekly newspaper. God is always more – more in scale, more in generosity, more in grace, more in forgiveness, more in ambition for humankind, more in uncalculating love. Just 'more'. Please let's not patronize God.

4 God loves life more than religion

We easily get hooked on religious activity rather than the redemption of the world. Again, it's a question of God's commitments being far greater than we imagine. Another quote from John V. Taylor:

It has long been my conviction that God is not hugely concerned as to whether we are religious or not. What matters to God, and matters supremely, is whether we are alive or not. If your religion brings you more fully to life, God will be in it; but if your religion inhibits your capacity for life or makes you run away from it, you may be sure that God is against it, just as Jesus was.[2]

We can live out our lives in tea spoons or in great handfuls, and I think I know what Jesus' preference would have been. He didn't say, 'I have come that they may be more religious,' or 'I have come that they may be more moral,' but 'I have come that they may have life and have it abundantly' (John 10.10).

This means that there is no part of life in which God is not interested. That comes as a surprise to some people who imagine that God is fundamentally religious and therefore concerned about the things with which religion is traditionally associated – prayer, worship on Sundays, good works, church organizations, upholding morality. But the God of Everything is bound to be fascinated by politics, mortgages, global trade, the latest films, prison reform, shopping, holidays, the nation's health, and so on – all the things that make for our well-being. And yes, God is committed to our full enjoyment of this extraordinary world too. One rabbi famously said that the first question he would be asked by God at the end of his life would be: 'Did you enjoy my creation?'

5 God is grace-full

Some people have God as a solitary, dominant power, primarily concerned with exerting the Divine Will on creation. The result is a flattened, restrictive, even bullying gospel which does no credit to anyone. An alternative vision is of God as unprotected generosity, enthusiastic encouragement, limitless possibility. This understanding of God is amazed at God's grace, the grace of a God who comes all the way to meet us, who showers us with gifts, and who invites us to inhabit a world of grace and favour. Grace seems to me to be the melody line of the New Testament; that's what we see being lived out in the life of Jesus. If only we could live more gracefully and generously; sadly we tend not to live too much of the gospel because it's simply too big, too radical and demands too much change.

God's graceful touch in our lives is like the 'first touch' of a skilled footballer. Such a player brings a ball down, controls it and distributes it, all in one elegant, flowing movement. God's first touch means that whatever we give him, God brings down, 'controls' and gives back. He takes it, makes it manageable, and gives it back; he takes it, makes it manageable, and gives it back. All the time. God never hangs on to the ball; he wants us to shine on the field of play, using the skills he has to teach us. God wants us to be as deft and joyous as Jesus, as warm and alive as love.

6 God is Christlike

If God is the graceful centre of reality, then he's demonstrated what that grace looks like in the person of Jesus. You can look at the life, character and teaching of Jesus of Nazareth and say, 'That's God for you.' In the abundance of fish caught when Simon Peter was fed up after fishing all night and catching only tiddlers; in the ridiculous quantity of wine that emerged late in the day at Cana; in the outrageous productivity of five loaves and two fishes at the end of a day's teaching; in rescuing a little man who'd lost his way collecting taxes for the occupying power; in the healing of a blind man selling the Palestinian equivalent of the *Big Issue* – in all these situations we might say: 'That's God for you.' That's what God is like.

If you were God and wanted to communicate with men and women you might send them messages through great people, or perhaps get prophets to tell them to smarten up their act, but finally you might have to send your own child who knows you through and through and who you can trust with complete confidence as your agent. That's what God did. Here is the one of whom you can say, 'Like Father, like Son,' the human face of God, God's self-portrait. It was Archbishop Michael Ramsey who said: 'God is Christlike and in him there is no unChristlikeness at all.'[3] That about sums it up.

7 God is obsessed with justice

To read the press, or even to listen in to internal church debates, you'd think God must be obsessed with sex (as if society isn't!). The reality is that God is obsessed with justice. The Bible has very little to say about personal sexual behaviour but a huge amount to say about the oppression of the poor, the exploitation of power and the responsibility of the rich. The Bible Society published a version of the Bible with every reference to these issues highlighted in blue, and the result is an eye-opener. God is the ultimate freedom fighter. His purpose is to 'let my people go' in order that they should experience the joyful freedom for which they were created.

Archbishop Desmond Tutu tells of a pedestrian crossing in apartheid South Africa which had a road sign that said: 'Danger, natives cross here.' Someone had mischievously altered the sign so that it now said: 'Danger, natives *very* cross here.' That is the authentic voice of those who seek justice, and it was the courageous stand of church leaders such as Desmond Tutu that led to him chairing the important South African Truth and Reconciliation Commission. The revealed character of God is clearly one of justice, and believers are bound to the same commitment.

8 God is always on your side

In his highly readable book *Ten Letters*, Chris Russell writes to a friend:

You are loved strongly and relentlessly, faithfully and without any reservation. Your God does not watch you undecided, he does not wait to be convinced, the jury is not out. The verdict in Christ is unflinching and irreversible. *He is for you.* Always. Without hesitation, deviation, but with endless repetition.[4]

This is the authentic message of the cross. God is prepared to do anything to demonstrate his commitment to our saving and well-being. As we look at the cross we see a great storm of horror, beauty and brilliance, but the underlying message is that God will not be shaken from his commitment to us, even by this terrible suffering.

There are times when all of us wonder who is there for us. We're struggling to stay afloat in some deeply challenging situation and as we look around for help, our supporters seem to have melted away. But there is One whose love is lashed to the mast, as it was once lashed to a cross. God will be there till we die or rise again. It's a promise I've found to be proven time and time again.

9 God suffers with you

It follows from the last paragraph that the God who is always on your side is also the God who will suffer with you when the dark wind is blowing straight in your face. In a sense all those who suffer (which means all people everywhere) find that there is no real explanation of suffering, only different ways of living with it. Most of the pain of the world is a consequence of God's decision to create a physical universe where accidents, collisions and compressions are inevitable. Given that awesome and wonderful decision, God does all that love can do; and as every parent knows, sometimes that means simply being alongside in anguished identification. Our comfort in suffering is that the Man of Sorrows is sure to pass this way. There's a statue in Chartres Cathedral, a beautiful depiction of God on the seventh day of creation. If you look carefully, there's one silent tear rolling down his face. God suffers with us, and our pain soaks into God's life as his life and strength soaks into ours.

Julian of Norwich, the fourteenth-century mystic, wrote of God's word to her in the midst of her intense exposure to God: 'He did not say, "You will not be troubled, you will not be belaboured, you will not be disquieted", but he said, "You will not be overcome."' That might be as far as God can go. God holds us in the palm of his hand but he necessarily holds us loosely and gently, not coercively. It's a holding that millions of us have trusted, and that trust has not been disappointed for he never lets us go.

10 God is always rising again

This is the amazing bit. Since the cosmic earthquake of the resurrection, the aftershocks just keep on happening and show no sign of dying away. It seems that the cross and resurrection are now scoured into the human landscape; we keep on coming to the end of the road and finding a new road has been built in a quite different direction. We're often told that you can't keep a good God down, but the proof of that somewhat clichéd expression is the personal experience of too many people to number. Priests and ministers across the land see a score of stories before them every time they look out on a congregation. They see faces marked by suffering but made beautiful by the overcoming of it. God is always on that search and rescue mission; indeed we go back to my first conviction about God, that *God is not somewhere else.* God is always on the job, characteristically raising the dead.

Story (familiar but worth repeating)

'Is – is he a man?' asked Lucy.

'Aslan a man!' said Mr Beaver sternly. 'Certainly not. I tell you he is the King of the wood and the son of the great

Emperor-beyond-the-sea. Don't you know who is the King of Beasts? Aslan is a lion – the Lion, the great Lion.'

'Ooh!' said Susan, 'I'd thought he was a man. Is he – quite safe? I shall feel rather nervous about meeting a lion.'

'That you will, dearie, and no mistake,' said Mrs Beaver. 'If there's anyone who can appear before Aslan without their knees knocking, they're either braver than most or else just silly.'

'Then he isn't safe?' said Lucy.

'Safe?' said Mr Beaver. 'Who said anything about safe? 'Course he isn't safe. But he's good.'[5]

Taking it further

Do these ten things I believe about God ring any bells? If so, we can rejoice together. If not, why not write your own? No right or wrong answers! As a wise priest used to say on one of my courses: 'Experience is sacred; interpretation is free.'

3

Ten things I don't believe about God

1 God is out to get you

It's fascinating how deeply embedded this belief about God is, even in the hidden crevices of believing minds. You can see where it comes from. None of us would be especially happy with a 24/7 video of our lives being played back to a select audience of, say, our life partner, children, a few journalists and the Archbishop of Canterbury. We all know we often do things that are shabby, think things that are dubious, and imagine things that are worse. Enlarge the audience to include a God who is ever present and said to be mega-righteous and you have a problem. Many people carry a hidden image of God as a celestial referee with his hand always on his back pocket where the yellow cards are kept.

Certainly God is always present but that presence is the sort you always want alongside you. God is like the loving parent at sports day, encouraging the beloved child to do her best, delighting in her successes and commiserating when she falls over at the start. And to those who believe God is itching to use the final red card to send us to the burning hot showers, I advise checking out the ways of Jesus. Jesus touched and healed anyone who came his way. There was no form to fill in, no CV to present. Why would Jesus' love be so unconditional in his life and ministry and so completely conditional afterwards? God is our greatest fan. He loves us to bits. He's not out to get us.

2 God is a tyrant

Activist Peter Tatchell was not in his most mellow mood when he wrote: 'The idea of God is synonymous with irrationality, superstition, ignorance, and usually dogmatism, insecurity, authoritarianism, intolerance, self-loathing and injustice. Religion has been mostly an instrument of war, bigotry and oppression.'[1] And that is what many believe – that God is a scary, irascible tyrant whose ways are cruel and whose goal is global domination. Some fear a clash of religious civilizations as different religious visions struggle for control, and they are not without evidence.

It's not an attractive picture of the faith and the God I have found to be life-giving. As ever, God gets landed with the excesses of religions shaped by human beings. Given that 'any thing you can understand cannot be God' (St Augustine), there are other metaphors that, for me, come much closer to describing the God who whispers in my inner and outer life: God as the Mysterious Laughter I hear in creation; God as the Gentle Persuader who touches me lightly on the shoulder; God as the Aching Beauty who speaks through nature and the arts; God as the Shimmering Presence always just beyond my reach but giving depth to common things. This is no terrorist but a God of infinite patience who isn't disturbed by our raucous denunciations, but continues to hold every one of us in the palm of his hand and as the apple of his eye. What incredible grace! Some religion is unhealthy; some is sublime; but God is constant and his name is Love.

3 God is arbitrary

Is the sun arbitrary? That's not hard to answer, but it's what some people would say of God, that his favour is distributed casually and unfairly, that he gave Jacob the breaks and turned his back on Esau, that he answers prayers in an inscrutable way, healing some and ignoring others. We loudly proclaim our 'God-incidences', while knowing that virtually every headstone is a symbol of unanswered prayer. I've prayed at the same time for people with similar diseases where one has died and the other lived. And we haven't even begun to quantify the vast disparity between being born into a middle-class Western family and being born into a family barely scraping a living on the edges of an African desert.

So is the sun arbitrary? No – but the effect of the sun is determined by many other factors, such as whether it's summer or winter, whether we are indoors or outdoors, under a tree or on a beach, in the Arctic or on the equator, and so on. The human condition is affected by a huge number of factors, not just the goodness of God. Moreover, we do need to usher offstage the concept of an all-controlling God who pulls the levers or operates the control switches on everything that happens. Such a God would have given us life in its worst form, with all the promise and none of the freedom. If we couldn't make our own decisions and determine our own destiny there would be no love, no courage, no mercy, no compassion, no success or failure – indeed nothing of true human value. If I fall off a bike I need to know that it has painful implications, not that I might bounce back up like a rubber ball. God is not arbitrary. And we have the unfathomable possibilities of prayer as well. As we pray we enlarge the space for God to be able to act, and when Love is released we can never know its limits.

4 God kills off his Son

Word has got around in some quarters that God had his Son killed in order to appease his sense of justice. There was so much evil committed by so many people that God had to have someone who would be a human sacrifice and take all that evil onto himself. It was a re-run of a bad movie from the

Old Testament when Abraham was told by God to take his son Isaac up into the hills and kill him, just to prove that Abraham could be relied upon. There was a reprieve, of course, but the very idea makes every parent shudder. So here is Jesus, strung up on a cross to satisfy an abstract principle that Justice must be fed an innocent victim every so often to balance the books.

That's the crude version. But scratch the surface of some theologies and the idea is still festering. The absolute antidote is found in Paul's assertion that 'God was in Christ, reconciling the world to himself' (2 Cor. 5.19, RSV). It was God himself who was taking the onslaught of hatred, violence and contempt, not the innocent Son of an angry Father. This is the love of a father who'll give his life for his family, of a teacher who'll lose her life to shield her young charges from a wild gunman, of a priest who'll take the place of another person in a queue entering a gas chamber. Evil is real; it has consequences and has to be dealt with. But it doesn't have to be 'bought off'; it has to be defeated. And that's what the cross was about.

5 God is on the defensive

Some Western commentators are daily writing God's obituary. Jamie Whyte is one. He says: 'How can it be that so many people continue to believe pre-Enlightenment gobbledegook? It is simply not possible for people who know as much as modern Westerners do to believe in the central tenets of Christianity or the other major religions.'[2] Julian Baggini agrees: 'In the scientific universe, God is squeezed until his pips squeak. For those without faith, that God [the one depicted on the ceiling of the Sistine Chapel] is clearly dead, and, yes, science helped to kill him.'[3]

God is long used to reading his own death notice and doesn't seem unduly bothered. No seven bowls of God's wrath, no end-of-the-world threats. God continues to love his world and to encourage his friends to do the same. I guess if you invented the whole universe, and it is sustained in being only because you believe in it, then you won't be too worried if some of the billions of folk on it are a wee bit rebellious. And anyway, there's always the 80 per cent of people of every race, culture, civilization and century who do believe that they live in a divine, transcendent context. In any case, rather than worry about his poll rating, God wants to get on with the major task of healing this beloved creation. He has bigger fish to fry.

6 *God is a clockmaker*

In arguing for the existence of God, William Paley (1743–1805) came up with what seemed to many like a knock-down proof. He suggested that if you came across a watch on the ground while walking on a heath, you wouldn't believe it could have come about by accident; you would know it had been made by a watchmaker. Similarly if you look at the intricacy of the universe you can't think it came about by accident either; it must have resulted from an Intelligent Designer: that is, God. This argument was largely displaced from theological debate after evolution and natural selection provided an alternative explanation for complexity and adaptation in the species. However, the argument refused to lie down, and it's alive again now, and in varying degrees of health, not only in the inadequate theology of creationists but more respectably in the argument developed from the anthropic principle, which starts with the observation that the world is incredibly and improbably fine-tuned for carbon-based life (see later). The philosopher Antony Flew famously revised his atheism late in life when he found that the evidence of design led him to belief in a creator God.

However, belief in a divine watchmaker, who winds up the clockwork at the start and then sits back to watch history unfold, will not do as an image of the God of the Abrahamic faiths. In these three great traditions God is utterly involved in his creation as the God of history and of personal behaviour. God is committed to his people's well-being and to interacting with them. He's always 'up close and personal'. The divine watch-maker is a pale imitation of the full-bodied God Christians see in Jesus. Indeed Jesus is the final evidence that God is passionately involved in searching out, healing and rescuing his people. God holds nothing back; for further details, see the cross.

7 God intends us to be literalists

One of the dispiriting features of some atheistic commentary on religion is its lack of subtlety. Academic Terry Eagleton began a famous review of Richard Dawkins' *The God Delusion* with these words: 'Imagine someone holding forth on biology whose only knowledge of the subject is the *Book of British Birds*, and you have a rough idea of what it feels like to read Richard Dawkins on theology.'[4] He is taking the writer to task for what he calls the 'vulgar caricatures of religious faith that would make a first year theology student wince'. It's easy to put up a straw man and then destroy him. 'What, one wonders, are Dawkins's views on the epistemological differences between Aquinas and Duns Scotus? Has he read Eriugena on subjectivity, Rahner on grace or Moltmann on hope? Has he even heard of them?'

A fundamentalist understanding of faith and a literalist reading of the Bible do no credit to the wonderfully sophisticated thinking about faith that has marked the Christian centuries. Moreover, the credibility of the Bible doesn't depend on the believability of Genesis or the edibility of Jonah. Some of the greatest minds in the world have worked on the Scriptures and found compelling truth at many levels. Richard Rohr says: 'I totally believe in Adam and Eve now, but on about ten more levels. Literalism is usually the lowest and least level of meaning.'[5] The Bible is an extraordinary set of books, written over 1,500 years by many different people in a kaleidoscope of genres, but all bearing witness to the faithfulness of God as men and women developed their understanding of his loving action in their lives and the life of nations. It's not an even-textured book. It has lumpy bits where the writers' understanding of God is embryonic. But it has golden themes of grace and love, of character and beauty, running through the whole, and it's been the cornerstone of civilizations and the foundation of countless lives. It must always be read with care, respect and an open mind. Literalism is a poor tool.

8 God is competitive

We live in a culture obsessed with numbers – hence the genesis of this book! – and this compulsive behaviour leads to competition over things like growth rates and market share. This easily slips over into the sphere of religious faith. Why otherwise do I know that there are 2.3 billion Christians in the world and 1.6 billion Muslims, or that there are 70,000 more Christians every day of the year? We might try and draw God into our minor obsessions were it not for the fact that God is plainly not interested. I want more people to discover the fulfilment of a personal faith (why would I not share the best thing I've found?) but it's not numbers in themselves that matter; it's the difference more people sharing that faith can make to the shaping of a flourishing, just and joyful world. I dare to think that that's also God's priority. The Kingdom of God isn't competitive, it's collaborative. It's a way of life in which your welfare is my concern, and mine is yours. In this way we forge communities of grace, generosity, participation and mutuality. The local church is a laboratory for this kind of living. Often it fails, but the point for society to note is that it sticks to the task. Where else does that happen? It starts with trying to imitate a God who isn't competitive but is always collaborative.

9 God is disengaged from real life

The central Christian doctrine of the incarnation says to the world that God is experienced, unshockable and profoundly down-to-earth. Getting involved in the daily realities of messy human behaviour might seem like an unnecessarily sacrificial step for the Lord of the Universe, but it's of the essence of what Christians believe about God. God is not disengaged; he's up to his elbows in the dirty water of humanity, and says it matters because matter matters. Christianity is the most material of faiths. All over the country, therefore, Christians (as well as those of other and of no faith) are running night shelters, food banks, street pastor schemes, credit unions, housing trusts, legal advice centres, support groups, youth projects, employment schemes, good neighbour projects, lunch clubs for the elderly and much more. These people are witnessing to a God who is not disengaged but profoundly involved in making a difference.

I wonder what people are asking for when they want religion to be disengaged from the public square and jammed into a private box. It would mean unlearning and unravelling our whole social environment. You would have to be very careful about art and music, about galleries to enter and choirs to join; secular ones are rare. You would have to avoid most of the great poets, playwrights and novelists – no Shakespeare, for example. Biblical allusions would have to be excised from our language, and Armistice Day parades and war memorials removed from view. Your system of ethics would have to be revised, especially human rights, together with your understanding of self-sacrifice, philanthropy and voluntary service. Our parliamentary democracy and our legal system would have to be reinvented. Oh, and we'd have to start from the year 0. Let's just admit it – Western culture is saturated with the Christian faith. God doesn't know how to stand back.

10 God is my personal deity

God is not my talisman, my possession, my genie of the lamp. I don't even have a part-share. The God of Life, the Universe and Everything can't be co-opted onto my team, even as Head Coach. God is Ultimate Freedom. We belong to God, not God to us. I wouldn't want it any other way.

Story: Hugo Gryn in Auschwitz

On that day [Yom Kippur] in 1944 I was at my place of work. Like many others, I fasted and cleared a little hiding place for myself among the stacks of insulation boards. I spent most of the usual working day there, not even emerging for the thin soup given to us at midday. I tried to remember as many of the prayers as I could and recited them, asking for God's forgiveness for promises made and not kept. But eventually I dissolved in crying. I must have sobbed for hours. Never before or since have I cried with such intensity and then I seemed to be granted a curious inner peace. Something of it is still with me. I believe God was also crying. And I understood a bit of the revelation that is implicit in Auschwitz. It is about man and his idols. God, the God of Abraham, could not abandon me, only I could abandon God. I would like you to understand that in that builder's yard on that Day of Atonement, I found God. But not the God I had childishly clung to. People sometimes ask me 'Where was God in Auschwitz?' I believe that God was there himself – violated and blasphemed. The real question is 'Where was man in Auschwitz?'[6]

Taking it further

Do these ten things make sense? If so, we're on the same page, though doubtless you would have said it differently. But if not, what would have been your ten 'not-beliefs'? Why not jot them down and compare them with others?

4

Ten words of wisdom

Some people say there is a God; others say there is no God. The truth probably lies somewhere in between.   *W. B. Yeats*

If there is no God, who opens the doors in supermarkets?
Patrick Murray

Yes I admit Jesus was Jewish – but only on his mother's side.
Archie Bunker

The Bible tells us to love our neighbours, and also to love our enemies; probably because they are generally the same people.
G. K. Chesterton

The English churchgoer prefers a severe preacher because he thinks a few home truths will do his neighbours no harm.
George Bernard Shaw

It is easier for a camel to pass through the eye of a needle if it is lightly greased.   *Kehlog Albran*

I don't believe in an afterlife, although I'm bringing a change of underwear.   *Woody Allen*

You're not an agnostic, Paddy. You're just a fat slob who's too lazy to go to Mass.   *Conor Cruise O'Brien*

As God once said, and I think rightly . . .   *Margaret Thatcher*

The better sort of cannibals have been Christian for many years and will not eat human flesh uncooked during Lent without special and costly dispensation from their bishop.   *Evelyn Waugh*

5

Ten reasons to believe in God

I've never assumed that belief in God is an easy ride. I inherited a questioning disposition and am regularly drawn back to look at foundational arguments about faith. I relish the religious debates that are renewed in each generation, and I value my initial legal training as a tool for my curiosity. But I know that intellectual discussion will only take me so far because finally you don't 'prove' people, you meet them; and that's what it's like with God. It's a different kind of knowledge, like the knowledge of the artist, the philosopher, the poet, the lover. Not superior to the knowledge of the physicist, the biologist and the biochemist, but different.[1] Nevertheless, let's see how far we can travel with human reason. Why believe in God?

1 Because you don't have to

The only God I could believe in is one who leaves it up to me whether I believe or not. If I was forced to believe by the sheer inescapable logic and necessity of it, I would cease to have that most essential human attribute – the freedom to make up my own mind. It would be like me making my children repeat a hundred times every night, 'My dad loves me,' rather than letting them discover it for themselves by the way I acted towards them. To be forced to believe would actually be coercive and the very opposite of the character of a loving parent or a loving God.

It would also mean that I had become superior to God because I would be the one who contained God in my own mind. I would be the possessor of the proof and God would be the one proved. To put it another way, to be able to prove the reality of God would be like Macbeth proving the reality of Shakespeare, which is of course logically impossible because Shakespeare and Macbeth exist in different planes – creator and created. Logically and of necessity God will always be beyond us.

Moreover, the reality of God will always be beyond human expression. Every description of God must be metaphorical. The philosopher Wittgenstein once poured a cup of freshly ground coffee and asked his students to describe the smell. They couldn't. So Wittgenstein said, in effect: 'If we haven't got words to describe the smell of coffee which we can hold in a cup in our hands, how can we think we have the words accurately to describe God?'

So we will never 'prove' the existence of God, or even speak of God adequately. All we can do is point to possible signs of divinity, and offer the invitation to 'taste and see'. We can look at the reasonableness of belief without attempting to produce any knock-down arguments. Different signs that might point to God can have a cumulative effect, but belief, and more especially faith, will always be a choice. Which explanation makes more sense?

2 Because it answers the question, 'Why is there something rather than nothing?'

This question is the basic puzzle of existence. It's the place where science, philosophy, theology and the human quest for meaning come together. The answer sometimes given, that the universe has always existed and never had a beginning, may or may not be true, but it's a cop-out; we're not dealing here with an inexorable chain of cause and effect, but rather with the way the great cosmic enterprise rests on the Divine Artist creating for the sheer hell of it (correction: the sheer love of it). This is a 'why' question more than a 'how' question, though the two overlap. In any case, God is not one object in a field of objects. God and the universe do not add up to two, any more than my pride and my appendix constitute a pair of objects. God is no-*thing*. He just is. God, as Christians understand God, is Being itself, the ground of all being, the condition of possibility for any form of existence at all. God isn't on any objective map but is the reason why there's a map at all and why there's anything on it. As St Bonaventure put it: 'God is a sphere whose centre is everywhere and whose circumference is nowhere.'[2]

Great minds are able to put things simply, so when the former Archbishop of Canterbury, Rowan Williams, was sent a letter in which a little girl called Lulu asked God how he got invented, he replied like this, answering on God's behalf:

> Dear Lulu, Nobody invented me, but lots of people discovered me and were quite surprised. They discovered me when they looked round at the world and thought it was really beautiful or really mysterious and wondered where it came from. They discovered me when they were very quiet on their own and felt a sort of peace and love they hadn't expected. Then they invented ideas about me, some of them sensible and some of them not very sensible. From time to time I sent them some hints – specially in the life of Jesus – to help them get closer to what I'm really like. But there was nothing and nobody around before me to invent me. Rather like somebody who writes a story in a book, I started making up the story of the world and eventually invented human beings like you who could ask me awkward questions . . .[3]

Why is there something rather than nothing? Perhaps because God wrote the story.

3 Because we know there's a difference between good and evil

We need some adequate grounding for the stubborn insistence of society that some things matter, and indeed have a right to matter; that some things aren't just a matter of preference but are objectively right and objectively wrong. It can't be said that child abuse, rape, genocide, torture, racism and the like are wrong just because most of us don't like them. When a homicidal gunman enters a school and kills 20 six- and seven-year-olds and their teachers, we can't say we don't like that sort of thing and wouldn't, personally, choose to do it. It's objectively and absolutely wrong. Similarly with the good that people like Gandhi, Mother Teresa and Nelson Mandela do – these are good at a level beyond personal preference. Certain situations confront us and make a claim on us, and have a right to do so. This isn't just a case of biological determinism with certain actions advancing the survival of the species and other actions damaging that survival. The unconditional claim of many moral actions goes beyond what is expedient for the human race and takes us into the arena of sacrifice and love for love's sake.

Where does this apparent 'objectivity' come from in the moral sphere? Talk about human nature or inherent rights seems at first to offer an explanation that doesn't have to veer off in the direction of God, but on closer examination these approaches emerge simply as what the philosopher Jeremy Bentham called 'nonsense on stilts', free-floating ideas that are good in themselves but without grounding. They're plucked from the air, or rather, they're taken, without acknowledgement, from the Judaeo-Christian tradition that has shaped the values of our society. It isn't enough to say that such behavioural truths are self-evident and now embodied in the UN Declaration of Human Rights. Those rights rest on a religious foundation which is at least consistent with belief in a moral Mind behind the universe.

4 Because belief is a universal human instinct

When the vast majority of human beings on earth, through every period of history, in every civilization and setting, agree on the same thing, you have to take notice. The 'thing' in question here is the reality of the transcendent as the context in which we live. This is obviously not to say that we have all believed in the same shape of that transcendence, but the belief that life is both spiritual and religious in character is a shared conviction across the face of the earth. This has been attributed to evolutionary need, psychological deficit and other alternative causes by those who don't share this perception of life, but reductionism (the tendency to reduce awkward phenomena to 'nothing but' something else) is a poor intellectual tool. Most common human experiences are matched by a reality that actually exists; so hunger corresponds to food, thirst to drink, and sexual desire to a sexual partner. Why should this not be so with the universal instinct of the numinous, the Other, God? The sacred fire burns within us. It seems that we might be born to believe.

5 Because of the experience of wonder

Who among us has not been stopped in our tracks by some experience so overwhelming that we had to simply shut up and stare? I lay in my sleeping bag under the stars in the Sinai desert and stared in amazement at the galaxy I usually couldn't see through the cloudy, light-polluted skies of the UK. I was vaguely aware that in our own homely little galaxy there are some 100,000 million stars like our sun, and this galaxy is one of 100,000 million other galaxies. But now, lying beneath this phenomenal sight, I was both reduced to silence and exhilarated beyond measure. 'What are human beings that you [God] are mindful of them?' (Ps. 8.4). Similarly, the knowledge that the human eye can distinguish between 7 million colours has me reaching for my chair. Apparently my brain processes more than a million messages a second, although my wife will vouch for it working well below capacity fairly often.

The experience of awe is universal. These are breathtaking moments that bless and burn. The movements of wildlife in a television programme on Africa; watching a small grandchild start using a crayon; exulting in a golden shaft of sunlight streaking through the dark clouds of winter. Sometimes it feels like our hearts will explode; sometimes we simply watch, silently amazed. For huge numbers of us these experiences of wonder take us beyond ourselves. There's something more than getting and spending and rushing and complaining. These are shining moments that point to new dimensions, just out of reach, almost beyond description, perhaps beyond sharing – but achingly desirable. What is the shimmering reality of which these moments are mere distant echoes? What do I do with wonder?

6 Because of the life, death and new life of Jesus

The one who has most completely drawn me to God is the person of Jesus. I had only glimpsed this Jesus out of the corner of my eye before I went to university. There he came fully into focus and formed the centre of my Christian vision, where he remains to delight and direct my faith. Rowan Williams wrote: 'Jesus is for Christians the one human agent who never blocks out the light, whose life and presence define holiness in each moment.'[4] His life, and in particular that tiny three-year segment we see in the Gospels, is one that has inspired, provoked, intrigued and thrilled more people than any other human being in history. Something totally remarkable was going on in that life and millions of people have named that otherness 'God'. God was going on in that life.

This is a life that hardly anyone has been able to fault. They might quibble, but from catacomb to papal palace, from Brazilian *favela* to Amalfi villa, from everywhere to everywhere, this life has reigned in the hearts of more people than we can number. The question has to be: if Jesus, who was so completely centred on his relationship with his heavenly Father, was so right in everything else he said and did, how could he have been so wrong in the basic truth on which he staked his life? If it comes down to it, I would rather trust Jesus on this than the doubts of my heart or the secular wisdom of the world. If he believed in God then so do I.

7 *Because of the impact of believers*

I nearly put: 'Because of the impact of the Church', but I know that for many of us that would be a mixed message. The Church hasn't been as reliable an agent of the life and love of God as any of us would want. That's simply because it's made up of people like me. But the Church nevertheless is a remarkable witness to something extraordinary. It was born in fear as angels and women tried to reassure 11 terrified disciples that Jesus had been raised from the dead. It then received a burst of amazing energy on the day called Pentecost, and went on to overturn most of the known world within three centuries. The Church now numbers a third of the world's population and is growing at a phenomenal rate.

Something has to account for all this. Could it all have been based on a mistake, a trick of the early morning light, credulous disciples, hallucination, wish fulfilment, then social reinforcement, political coercion and simple gullibility? Hardly. Not across so many centuries, for so many billions of people, for so long. Not across so many minds, brilliant, forensic, simple, devout. Not a hoax on such a gigantic scale. Something sufficient has to account for this.

The impact of the Church and the individual lives of which it is made up, has had a mixed record. I don't need to list the devastation that has sometimes been caused by bad theology and misguided humanity. However, the other record, of social justice, humanitarian reform, charitable activity, and sheer goodness at the level of a million daily details, is a colossal tribute to the transforming power of the gospel. Again, something sufficient has to account for this. Shall we say – the presence of God?

8 Because of personal experience

This is where I run the risk of hopeless subjectivism. However, unless I call to the bar the personal testimony of the communion of saints, alive and what we call 'dead', I will be selling the evidence short. If people like me and millions of others maintain that they have in some way encountered God, that experience has to be evaluated and given some weight. Of course, if the issue has already been decided on an *a priori* basis then nothing in this area of human experience can count as evidence. But if not, then we need to consider why, when regular churchgoing in the West is not as strong as it was, the number of people reporting they have had a spiritual or religious experience (suitably defined) has risen remarkably. Such self-descriptions run the risk of ridicule, with the result that few people are prepared to admit the experiences to their friends, but in reputable surveys and under rigorous academic scrutiny the story is different – and shocking to the secular mind. We have to remember the problem that if we talk to God it's called prayer but if God talks to us it's called mental illness. Nevertheless the characteristic Christian experience is that we have, from time to time, encountered something more than the here and now, something utterly loving and transforming. Someone many people call God.

Writer Francis Spufford is unashamedly bullish about personal experience in his exhilarating book *Unapologetic*, where he defends what he calls 'the intelligibility, the grown-up dignity of Christian emotions'. In a culture where the God question is usually confined to barren intellectual bombardment, he wanted to write about what faith feels like from the inside. He writes: 'It is a mistake to suppose that it is assent to the propositions that makes you a believer. It is the feelings themselves that are primary. I assent to the ideas because I have the feelings; I do not have the feelings because I assent to the ideas.'[5] He may be right, but of course the two are interdependent.

What matters here is to affirm that human testimony to the divine has to be given house-room in our thinking about the reasonableness of belief in God.

9 Because it makes more sense of more things more of the time than any other explanation

If I'm looking for a Grand Unifying Theory I can look in two places: to theoretical physicists and to theologians. They think big thoughts and often those thoughts are surprisingly similar. Or perhaps not surprisingly. God's world is one world; we just have different descriptive languages. I value hugely all that science can tell me of ultimate things. I can enjoy these explorations and findings to the full. But to give a final account of the universe in all its richness, I find myself saying, 'I believe in God.'

10 Because it's the best story

In Yann Martel's book *Life of Pi*,[6] the ship in which young Pi and his family are sailing sinks in a storm and the young hero has an incredible voyage in the company of a Bengal tiger called Richard Parker. He barely survives, but in his hospital bed he has to give an account of what has happened to two insurance agents. He tells the story of his remarkable relationship with the tiger and finds his listeners totally disbelieving, so he tells them a much more conventional story of what happened, full of human cruelty. At the end of the two accounts the young man poses the vital question to his listeners: 'Which story do you prefer?'

That's it for us too. Which story do we prefer? Is it God or no-God? Which story makes most sense? Both are believable; both have their strong points. No one can prove beyond doubt that either is the truth. We have to decide which is the better story for us to live by. For all the reasons in the rest of this chapter I'm convinced by the God story, but we can't put the evidence under a microscope in the laboratory. Ultimately it's an informed choice.

Which story do you prefer?

Story

A young fish was enjoying himself swimming around the ocean and sometimes talking to a wise old fish. One day he asked him: 'Where's the ocean? I hear other fish talking about it but no one ever says where it is.'

The wise old fish smiled and said: 'Why, you're already in the ocean. It's right here all around you.'

'No,' said the little fish, 'this is only water. I want to know where the ocean is.' And he swam off, disappointed.

Taking it further

Which of the ten reasons do you think are most helpful and which most contentious? How could they be improved? What arguments have you used when talking to someone who doesn't believe in God?

6

Ten beliefs about science and religion

————•◦•————

Let's be clear straight off. My formal scientific education ended a very long time ago, so proper scientists beware. But the issues of science and faith are crucial to any adult believer with an intelligent faith in modern times. What follows are the doubtless scrambled thoughts of a Christian who has long been fascinated with the debate but claims no expertise. I'm like the man who said to the vicar as he left church: 'Thank you for that sermon, vicar. I've never understood that subject, and I still don't understand it – but at a higher level.' On the other hand, ordinary people like me need the freedom to talk about science as interested members of the community, in the same way that we can offer opinions about music, art, drama or television programmes. Science, too, is a shared human endeavour.

1 The conflict model is unnecessary

The media delights to present the relationship of science and religion as necessarily conflictual. But this has not been the norm historically, nor is it necessary today. Religious belief functioned as the framework that nurtured the birth of Western science. Belief in the unity and consistency of God made possible the rational exploration of the physical world. The Church's treatment of Galileo is often portrayed as the normal stance of religion to progressive science, ignoring the fact that this was an idiosyncratic event reflecting an internal struggle within the faith to which Galileo remained true all his life as he tried to help his own church develop its thinking. As modern science emerged in seventeenth-century Europe, almost without exception the 'natural philosophers' (the scientists) were either devout or conventionally religious.[1] When T. H. Huxley and Bishop Samuel Wilberforce had their famous debate in Oxford in 1860, at which the latter raised the question of whether the descent of Huxley from a monkey had been on his grandmother's or grandfather's side, the idea of evolution was warmly welcomed by many Christians, including writer Charles Kingsley and the future Archbishop of Canterbury Frederick Temple.[2]

The more normal response of faith to scientific enquiry is represented by Johannes Kepler, the seventeenth-century mathematician and astronomer, who said unequivocally: 'God is being celebrated in astronomy.' The large numbers of Christians who work in or teach science would take the same view of their disciplines. The search for truth is absolutely essential to both science and faith. Indeed, Dominican writer Timothy Radcliffe put it like this: 'A society which loses confidence in the very possibility of truth ultimately disintegrates. Augustine called humanity the "community of truth". It's the only basis upon which we may belong to each other.'[3] A conflict model between these two great interrelated traditions doesn't help anyone, nor is it necessary.

2 Science and theology are complementary, but not independent, languages

A common distinction between the tasks of science and theology says that science answers the 'how' questions and theology the 'why' questions. When observing a boiling kettle you can describe in molecular terms the change of water into steam as boiling point approaches, or you can say that someone must be making a cup of tea. Jonathan Sacks expressed the complementarity like this: 'Science takes things apart to see how they work. Religion puts things together to see what they mean.'[4] This is an oversimplification, of course, because science also puts things together and has spawned the likes of systems theory and complexity theory. Nevertheless it starts the discussion. The 'how–why' distinction is another form of the 'non-overlapping magisteria' (NOMA) of Harvard scientist Stephen Jay Gould, who proposed it as a way of avoiding argument and keeping the peace: 'The net of science covers the empirical universe: what is it made of (fact), and why does it work this way (theory). The net of religion extends over questions of moral meaning and value.'[5] This gets the discussion out of the starting blocks in that it offers full respect to both languages and ensures that one discipline doesn't try to trump the other. However, the question we're left with is whether this approach goes far enough, and whether it oversimplifies and closes down the potential fruitfulness of the discussion. Science isn't only concerned with factual knowledge, just as religion isn't only concerned with values and morals. These languages may be complementary but they're not completely independent.

3 Science and religion give each other important tools to do their jobs

This is a richer representation of the relationship between science and faith. It goes beyond the dualism of NOMA and recognizes that there is just one world, and to describe it adequately requires a unity of knowledge. Religion and science both tackle the biggest questions of existence. They're concerned with understanding the nature of the universe, its origins and purpose. We live in a world where scientific presuppositions come as standard; they're in the very air our culture breathes. No religion that attempts to offer interpretation and guidance to the societies in which it is set can possibly manage that task without integrating a scientific world-view into its own.

At the same time, science is advancing so fast, and technology is making so much possible so quickly, that there's a need for deep, tested, human wisdom to examine the ethical implications of these discoveries. The traditions of science and religion therefore need each other. People of faith need to be more humble – after all, the more we know, the bigger God gets. But the same applies to scientists; the scientific method doesn't provide a way of answering every question about ethics and human flourishing. Our world is full of enormous possibility today, for huge benefit and complete disaster, and we need everyone on board if we're to sail safely through these magnificent, terrifying seas. We may have complementary languages, but they serve each other in very significant ways as we attend to the same realities.

4 Pointers not proofs (i): the existence of anything rather than nothing

I've asked this question elsewhere in this book but it deserves a mention here because this is a key area where science and religion are treading over the same ground. The laws of physics obviously start operating in ways that are understood, from just a nanosecond after the Big Bang 13.7 billion years ago. The search continues for answers to why and how the original explosion occurred and here you have to posit either a creator, or a regress of causes, or a universe that is ultimately uncaused (though saying, 'There's no answer to this question', is often really a way of saying, 'There is an answer but I don't like it'). One alternative to the creator thesis, therefore, is a further cause – fluctuations in the quantum vacuum which then triggered the Big Bang – but this only pushes the problem a stage further back. Ultimately you are up against a philosophical question of how something can come out of nothing. The word 'metaphysics' may be unpopular with some scientists, but try substituting the word 'world-view'. Every metaphysical scheme/world-view has its unexplained foundation. We all start somewhere. The materialist starts with the existence of matter; the theist starts with the existence of a divine creator. Which makes most sense is a question we each have to answer.

5 Pointers not proofs (ii): the anthropic principle

It has long been observed that the universe is extraordinarily fine-tuned for carbon-based life. For example, if the speed of expansion from the initial singularity in the Big Bang had been infinitesimally faster or slower than it was, the universe would have either shot to pieces or collapsed in on itself. (This is layman's language, you understand.) There are a number of these pin-point accuracies which seem to depend on six apparently fundamental constants in nature. Someone suggested that the accuracy of just one of these parameters is comparable to getting the mix of flour and sugar right to within one grain of sugar in a cake ten times the mass of the sun. Our universe is 'just right' for life.

However, although astronomer Sir Fred Hoyle said that nothing had done more than this fine-tuning of the universe to undermine his atheism, it's important not to get carried away by the theological potential of these remarkable characteristics. There are other possible explanations apart from divine purpose. The main one is the existence of a vast number of universes, a 'multiverse', one of which, by sheer trial and error, is bound to have this possibility of carbon-based life. Or the universe might have expanded and contracted a huge number of times, but each time with slightly different parameters, and thus eventually it would have had the right set of values for life to emerge. But, of course, it could be said of this multiverse approach that if you can posit 10 to the 500th other universes to explain away otherwise inconvenient observations (the anthropic coincidences), you can explain away anything, and science itself becomes impossible. We have no scientific evidence to go on here. Physics has really left the room and metaphysics has taken over. More importantly, even if the multiverse theory is true (and it might be), you are still left with the fine-tuning of a multiverse in which this kind of 'cosmic natural selection' could take place. You've merely pushed the puzzle a stage further back. Might Divine Will be a factor, and a much simpler explanation?

6 Pointers not proofs (iii): intelligibility

There's actually another fundamental issue to face. Why is the universe intelligible to us at all? Why does the rationality of the universe correspond to the rationality of our minds so that we can think about any of this? Einstein said that the most incomprehensible thing about the universe is that it's comprehensible. Moreover, the key to unlocking these cosmic secrets turns out to be mathematics, and mathematical equations have an economy and elegance that demonstrate that we have a universe that is not only rationally transparent but rationally beautiful. As John Polkinghorne writes:

> The profound intelligibility of the universe is a significant and mysterious fact. Those who are imbued with a deep thirst for understanding will not be content to treat it simply as a fortunate accident. We are driven to ask why the world is so beautifully and fruitfully ordered.[6]

7 Pointers not proofs (iv): wonder, love and purpose

I was at a conference on cosmology and theology and two distinguished professors of physics spoke of 'Oh, wow!' moments. This is another part of the common language of science and faith. There are heart-stopping moments when scale, beauty, elegance, symmetry, or whatever it is, evokes a sense of wonder and almost joy. To the believer it's the experience of knocking on the door of the divine. Truly, 'the heavens are telling the glory of God' (Ps. 19.1). The idea of purpose is also one that is difficult to expunge from people's vocabulary. Their lives and that of the universe seem to require some concept of movement towards a goal or an end. Stranger still, there is also, for many people, a dim perception of something at the heart of reality which is best described by the word 'love'. The theme of *co-operation* runs deeply through biology and it has been suggested that it could be one of the basic principles of evolution.[7] None of these concepts of wonder, purpose and love is an obviously scientific one, but each seems ineradicable in human experience, and sometimes to be echoed faintly in scientific discussion. Again, the languages may be complementary but in places they also overlap. And Christians want to know why they seem to be carved so deeply into the way we experience life.

8 Christ is at the centre of a Christian understanding of creation

We're now stretching scientific credulity to the limit. But no Christian doctrine of creation can function without the high claims of the New Testament that Christ is at the heart of creation. The cosmic significance that Christ is given in the letters of Paul and the Gospel of John is always breathtaking. 'All things came into being through him and without him not one thing came into being' (John 1.3). 'In him all things in heaven and on earth were created, things visible and invisible . . . all things have been created through him and for him . . . in him all things hold together' (Col. 1.16–17). And Christ is key to the present and future as well as the past: 'If anyone is in Christ there is a new creation: everything old has passed away; see, everything has become new' (2 Cor. 5.17).

What this insistence tells us is that having a Creator is not enough; we need to know who the Creator is. Revelation therefore completes nature. It isn't sufficient to get sucked into a deistic discussion of God as the initial Creator. That isn't the

Christian understanding of creation at all. Christians see God as sustaining all creation all the time, not lighting the blue touchpaper and stepping back. And the instrument of his sustaining power is the divine energy of the cosmic Christ, who touched the earth decisively in the person of Jesus of Nazareth.

9 Evolution fits the facts

The resistance of some fundamentalists to evolution and its replacement with creationism, or its younger brother 'intelligent design', does a tragic disservice to a sensible debate between science and religion. It suggests that Christian believers are intellectually underdeveloped and that religion can be ignored as a serious contributor to intelligent debate. This baleful project of putting evolution and creationism in opposition to each other only emerged significantly in the 1960s and it means that all sorts of important words like 'creation' and 'design' – even 'intelligent' – have effectively been hijacked. The fact is that evolution fits the facts – overwhelmingly. Believing in evolution doesn't in any way necessitate atheism; Darwin himself was at pains to make that clear. But the interplay of chance (what actually happens) and necessity (the context of 'laws' and regularities) allows new things to emerge. Order and openness interact creatively in a way they couldn't if things were either too rigid or too haphazard. As it is, the vastly complex interplay of nature has, through natural selection, resulted in you and me, and the wonderful – but costly – potentialities of the future. God has given creation the open opportunities (chance) and the stable regularities (necessity) through which the world can make itself in freedom.

Of course, this also gives us a way of understanding the Christian believer's greatest problem, that of explaining pain and suffering. There appears to be no better way to allow life to make itself than by evolution through natural selection. This radical freedom is given to all of life at every level of material being – to humans who may love or hate, to cells that may replicate for health or for cancer, to tectonic plates that may create continents or cause tsunamis, and so on. The love of God is such that in creating a world of freedoms he limits his power in the interests of love. That's what love always does. Parents limit their raw authority in order to enable their children to grow up as mature, loved and loving adults. Teachers create environments that combine freedom and structure, to enable their students to explore knowledge and ideas. Love always exercises self-restraint. The results may sometimes be disastrous, but it's the only way for those consequences to be amazing as well. Evolution – and life – is tough, wasteful and sometimes horrific, but that's the cost of a world that's worth it and not a world run by a divine puppeteer.

10 Science is a Christian vocation

How is it that a congregation gets very excited when a young person goes off to theological college in order to be ordained, but says a much more muted farewell to another young person going off to university to read physics? Why does there seem to be a hierarchy of spiritual value going down from saints (rare) through monks, clergy, teachers and doctors, to social workers, police and other caring professions, but thereby relegating all other Christians as also-rans? Science used to be seen as a religious vocation, a thread that can be seen from medieval times and strongly found in Islamic thought too. Scientists are undertaking the wonderful task of 'thinking God's thoughts after him' and discovering ever more fascinating and potentially fruitful information about the way the world is – the world that is God's. Scientists are pursuing one of the vital tasks given to us – that of replacing darkness with light, ignorance with wisdom. All creation groans for salvation, according to Paul in Romans 8, so science has a major part to play in 'God's Great Project'. Fortunately, in spite of being ignored by much church life, some Christians who have a career in science are able to see the significance of what they are doing. Francis Collins, who used to be Director of the Human Genome Project, said: 'The work of a scientist involved in this project, particularly a scientist who has the joy of also being a Christian, is a work of discovery which can also be a form of worship.' That's the authentic voice of science offered back to God. Please can we give such encouragement and affirmation to that young person going off to read physics as well?

Story

The visionary poet William Blake was once asked whether, when he saw the sun setting, he did not see a ball of fire about the size of a guinea. 'Oh, no,' he replied, 'I see a multitude of the heavenly host crying, "Holy, holy, holy is the Lord God Almighty".'

Taking it further

What are the major questions you would like to ask scientists? You could make a list of them and invite someone in your church who is a practising scientist or teaches science to come and answer them. Alternatively, there's a huge literature on the subject of science and religion (look out for the names John Polkinghorne, Francis Collins, Denis Alexander, David Wilkinson, Keith Ward, Tom McLeish) and members of the group could go and research some answers.

7

Ten Bible passages that tell the whole story

———◆•◆•◆———

We tend to encounter the Bible in puzzling, bite-sized bits. On the day I'm writing this, the readings at Morning Prayer bring us a passage from Isaiah 64 calling on God to 'tear open the heavens and come down', and a reading from 1 John 4 calling on us to 'love one another, because love is from God'. We could also have Psalm 73, which reminds us that 'truly God is good to the upright'. It's all splendid stuff but it's not very easy to understand the purpose of each reading, its context, and its relationship to the others. What we miss is the Big Story, the overarching narrative into which each part fits. Is it possible to see the grand narrative in ten passages? What follows is an attempt to offer just that, and to use 'friendship' as a binding metaphor to illustrate the golden thread that holds it all together.

1 Genesis 1.1—2.3: friendship formed

This is the great poetry of creation. How else could the writers describe that event, starting 14 billion years ago, when the first infinitesimally small singularity began its evolutionary journey? The writers wanted us to know that everything rests in God's creative pleasure, that he saw it all and smiled, because it was very good. And then he rested. It's not meant to be even embryonic science; it's bigger than that. It's the kind of poetry that tells the truth to every age and culture, and gives us room to understand ourselves. Here's a modern writer's equivalent, another poetic description of an event and process that lies beyond most minds, but embraces us all.

> Let me tell you why God made the world. One afternoon, before anything was made, God the Father, God the Son and God the Holy Spirit sat around in the unity of the Godhead discussing one of the Father's fixations. From all eternity, it seems, he had this thing about being. He would keep thinking up all kinds of unnecessary things – new ways of being and new kinds of things to be. And as they talked, God the Son suddenly said, 'Really, this is absolutely great stuff. Why don't I go out and mix us up a batch?' And God the Holy Spirit says, 'Terrific! I'll help you.' So they all pitched in, and after supper that night, the Son and the Holy Spirit put on this tremendous show of being for the Father. It was full of water and light and frogs; pine cones kept dropping all over the place and crazy fish swam around in the wineglasses. There were mushrooms and grapes, horseradishes and tigers – and men and women everywhere to taste them, to juggle them, to join them and to love them. And God the Father looked at the whole wild party and said, 'Wonderful! Just what I had in mind!'[1]

'God saw everything that he had made, and indeed, it was very good.' God's friendship with creation and with humankind was being formed.

2 Genesis 3: friends fall out

The poet now gives an account of why our best-laid plans fail and why our experience of life is so hard. Adam, the arche-typal person, is enticed by his partner to usurp his God-given limitations and to be like God. This is a step too far and it has tragic consequences for the woman, the man and the nefarious serpent. The woman will find childbirth painful and she won't be equal to her partner. The man will find work a struggle and a curse. And the serpent will have to slide over the ground rather than look over the hedge. Again, it's a wonderful piece of picture language, a cartoon, of the human condition. The message is: 'It isn't meant to be like this.' But the message is also: 'Don't worry. God is coming to look for you to bring you home.' When God says to the man and the woman, 'Where are you?' we're hearing the opening line of the great love story that is the Bible. Throughout the Scriptures we need to remember this central theme: this is God's search and rescue mission, motivated by love. The friendship may have been damaged, but one party of the friendship won't rest until he's brought his loved ones home.

3 Exodus 20.1–21: friends living together

We now enter the hazy territory where pre-history and real history merge in a complex way. The narrative vehicle is an account of the people of God being taken through a long, purgative experience of training in wild country on their way to their promised land. God needs to teach them how to live together positively, and his instructions and advice are focused in the Ten Commandments given to Moses in the inconvenient form of large stones he has to carry down the mountain and drop in front of his rebellious people. 'There's lots more where that came from', would be a suitable caption. (The rest of Exodus and Leviticus show that he wouldn't have been joking.) But what we see here is God the Lover teaching his undisciplined family how to live in ways that will enable them to flourish, to avoid damaging each other, and to relate effectively to both God their Protector and the rest of the human family. In effect he's saying: 'We're in this for the long haul. Let's smarten up and get some ground rules that'll work.' These friends, both divine and human, have to learn to live together, and as we've found ever since, this is the toughest task of all. Jesus tries a different approach in the Sermon on the Mount. The perennial question is always: how then shall we live? Humankind would do well to listen to the Ten Commandments; such wisdom isn't cheap. It reminds me of the assertion of G. K. Chesterton: 'Christianity has not been tried and found wanting; it has been found difficult and not tried.'[2]

4 Isaiah 11.1–9: friends look to the future

After struggling, for goodness knows how long, with this idea of 'friends living together', and after finding that various forms of leadership (judges, kings, a coalition) just didn't seem to work, God starts to send in some rather difficult characters to come at the problem from left field. They came in the context of Israel and Judah being thoroughly defeated by the Assyrians and Babylonians and going into a traumatic Exile. These disturbing people were the prophets – depressives like Jeremiah, weird ones like Ezekiel, hard-hitters like Amos, and an A-list prophet called Isaiah (well, there were probably three of them but we won't go into that). Isaiah was wonderfully prescient in seeing that the hopes of the nation and her God would eventually come down to rest on a single set of shoulders. 'A shoot shall come out from the stock of Jesse . . . The spirit of the Lord shall rest on him.' Later on, Isaiah would show even more breathtaking insight when he saw that the way God's search and rescue had to happen would be through the suffering of his Servant who would be despised and rejected and bear the sin of many (Isa. 53.3, 12). These prophets were a tough bunch but they always included in their message the golden thread of God's love story. God would stop at nothing to bring his friends home, so back they came from Exile to rebuild sacred Jerusalem.

5 John 1.1–18: friends start again

I always tremble with anticipation before the reading of John 1 at Midnight Communion. This magisterial passage has all the dignity and power necessary to announce the second creation story – which John clearly has in view. 'In the beginning . . . God created the heavens and the earth'; 'In the beginning was the Word . . .' The parallel is clear. The claims of these verses are quite staggering. 'He was in the beginning with God. All things came into being through him'; 'to all who received him . . . he gave power to become children of God'; 'And the Word became flesh and lived among us'. And all this was based on a fellow Galilean with whom the disciples had shared barbecues and played touch rugby on the beach. The hopes God had for a faithful nation of loyal friends had come down to a single life. This was the light that now shone in the darkness and that the darkness couldn't overcome. God was starting again with his friends. From the same source came the astonishment of the first letter of John, which starts with a similar sense of amazement. 'We declare to you what was from the beginning, what we have heard, what we have seen with our eyes, what we have looked at and touched with our hands . . .' You can almost hear him: 'Honest – I kid you not!' And we have this strange feeling that this is where we come in; this is when we can creep in and get some purchase on the story. God is approaching us too, and somehow asking for our friendship.

6 Matthew 5: friends learning together

One of the problems of a church year that majors on Christmas and Easter is that there isn't enough time in between. But into those few weeks we have to pack the whole of Jesus' ministry of teaching, healing and generally disturbing the peace. Jesus captivated his hearers with teaching that came fresh from the corridors of heaven and yet was completely earthed in the realities of everyday life. Matthew chapter 5 is part of what we call the Sermon on the Mount, a representative collection of his talks, Q and A sessions, and after-dinner speeches. What he says seems laughably impossible – 'If your right hand causes you to sin, cut it off'; 'If anyone strikes you on the right cheek, turn the other also'; 'Everyone who looks at a woman with lust has already committed adultery with her'. It's so ridiculous you just have to take it seriously. What is he doing? He's showing us that we've got so used to living upside down we don't even realize we're doing it. And this new upside-down, right-way-up world is starting to come true around him and his ministry. This is a public announcement, not a general truth about life. But what a challenge! We've grappled with this enigmatic teaching for centuries – which is just what Jesus would have wanted. He throws in crazy, tantalizing brain-teasers and says: play with that, think it through and let's see what comes out. This is how the friends of God learn; not by being told the answers before we've seen the questions, but by being fed the puzzles and encouraged to work on them. We've been learning together ever since.

7 Mark 15: our best Friend dying

If ever people ask how to start reading the Bible I tell them to read Mark's Gospel. What happens in the last two chapters (and I would ask them to supplement Mark's account of the resurrection with either Luke's or John's) is the centrepiece of history, the hinge on which everything turns. Every great love story has a crisis. God's search and rescue love story has now come to this and we watch, amazed, at the outworking of such humility. At the human level, this is what happens when sheer, unguarded goodness operates in a world of shabby compromise, political expediency and religious self-interest. Humankind can't stand too much goodness; we have to get rid of it because it shows us up too much. But Jesus kept on coming at the authorities and they just wanted to get rid of this troublesome prophet. At the divine level, God was in Christ offering himself and all he stood for to the world he loved. The Kingdom was theirs to enter; its framework had been sketched out by Jesus; did they want it? He waited. And we know the answer. 'Then Jesus gave a loud cry and breathed his last.'

8 Luke 24: friends on the road

Two friends on the road, walking in the wrong direction, away from the scene of the crime. A stranger falls in step with them and they share their depression and the collapse of their dreams. They arrive; a moment of hesitation; a meal. Bread is blessed, broken, shared. Suddenly, everything lurches wildly out of control; they grab for their scattered senses. How is this possible? But this is the Moment. 'Christianity is the only major faith built entirely around a single historical claim.'[3] And this is it. Christ is raised from the dead.

It's immensely comforting that the two friends were walking in the wrong direction, because that's what most of us do most of the time. The narrative of the Great Love Story is clear: God has been pursuing us since the beginning, whichever road we've been on and whichever direction we've been heading. He has invited us like a friend, seduced us like a lover, cajoled us like a teacher, warned us like a prophet – but eventually he's had to enter our experience like a Son, and that Son has gone to the ends of the earth for us, the end of his earthly life. But (the greatest word in the Bible) you can't destroy Love. Not if God is love and love is the energy of creation. How can love be turned off, shut down? In the resurrection the great engines of creation were thrown into reverse. Love is come again.

9 Second Corinthians 5: friends made new

One of the verses by which I have lived as a Christian has been verse 17 of this wonderful chapter. 'If anyone is in Christ, there is a new creation: everything old has passed away; see, everything has become new!' This exactly corresponded to my experience when first becoming a Christian in a meaningful way, and it has continued to speak to me, even when my discipleship has become a bit mundane and needing an injection of energy. Paul had been stopped in his tracks on a famous road trip to Damascus and his sense of wonder at this transformation always permeated his ministry and the theology he did on the run. All around him he saw people being made new, being transformed by the renewing of their minds (Rom. 12.2). They stood in a different relation to God and to each other. Because they had been raised with Christ they were to seek the things that are above and to set their minds there (Col. 3.1). The atmosphere of Paul's letters, and (though somewhat later) of Luke's narrative in the Acts of the Apostles, is full of fresh discovery and the shock of the new. Such buoyant young churches were bound to get into conflict and confusion and Paul is regularly having to try and fix a problem through his presence and his correspondence. Indeed, all his letters are addressing some problem or other; he doesn't seem to have written many 'Happy Birthday' letters or 'wish you were here' postcards. But this Church that he and others were founding, guiding and cherishing was the Church that changed the face of the world in just a few generations. Vulnerable, semi-skilled, apparently powerless, these Christians nevertheless proved irrepressible because they had within them a strength beyond human understanding. They were quite simply 'a new creation'.

10 Revelation 21: friends for ever

The end of the Big Story has to have the same poetic quality as the beginning. How can the mysteries of creation and the final curtain be understood, let alone accurately expressed, in ordinary flat language? On the island of Patmos, John saw a new heaven and a new earth, for the first heaven and the first earth had passed away. He saw the holy city, the new Jerusalem, coming down out of heaven from God. He heard the one seated on the throne say: 'See, I am making all things new.' He saw that the city had no need of sun or moon for the glory of God was its light, and its gates were never shut. This isn't the stuff you read in computer manuals or on cereal packets. But it has to be different because it's trying to express the inexpressible. The end of the Story is known to no one. Even Jesus said he didn't know what would happen. But Christians are confident, on the basis of all that God has done and shown himself to be, that all things will be gathered up in Christ and presented safely to God, who holds the original designs and has faithfully followed up the multiple twists and turns of his friends and their wilder passions. At the end we'll see that he's taken all we've done, undone and not done, and worked it into a fabulous fabric of beauty and love. OK, it's all poetic language – but what else can you do? The important thing is that God will have gathered up his friends for ever.

Quote: St John Chrysostom (fourth-century preacher)

Don't just listen carefully to what the preacher says, but take time regularly to read the Bible at home as well. Don't let anyone make excuses like these: 'I'm too busy with politics', 'I've got this or that public duty to fulfil', 'I'm a skilled worker, I must get on with my job', 'I've a wife and children to feed, I must provide for my family'; in other words, 'I'm a layman, it's not my business to read the Bible, I'll leave that to professional Christians like monks, nuns, priests and theology students.' What on earth are you saying? It's 'not your business to read the Bible' because you've got too many other things to bother about? But that's the very reason you need to read the Bible! The more worries you have, the more you need the Bible to keep you going. You are in the middle of the godless world's stormy sea, and so you need spiritual help and sustenance far more urgently. Monks and nuns live far from the battlefield but you are on the front line, face to face with the enemy, and you're bound to suffer frequent blows and be severely wounded. So you need the medicine chest close at hand . . . Haven't you noticed how a smith, mason or carpenter, or any other crafts-man, however much his back is against the wall, will never sell or pawn the tools of his trade? If he did, how could he earn his living? That's how we should think of the Bible; just as mallets, hammers, saws, chisels, axes and hatchets are the tools of the craftsman's trade, so the books of the prophets and apostles, and all scripture inspired by the Holy Spirit, are the tools of our salvation.[4]

Taking it further

Those are my ten passages telling the Big Story of the Bible. What do you think? Would you have chosen those? Why, or why not? Could you or your group prepare a different list and think through the reasons? Digging into this treasure store is always time well spent.

8

Ten key beliefs about Jesus

I'd seen Jesus in the distance many times before we were properly introduced. I'd got him down as a misty-eyed dreamer who dished out good advice about living and came to a very sticky end. I certainly hadn't seen him as the central figure of my life. It was while I was away at university that I realized that my understanding of Christianity was letting me see the debris of faith lying all over the place, without letting me see the explosion that had caused it in the first place. The explosion was Jesus Christ. Once you see that, everything else fits into place, including what we might make of this man ourselves. Rowan Williams puts it with characteristic accuracy:

> Only three human individuals are mentioned in the Nicene Creed, Jesus, Mary and Pontius Pilate: Jesus; the one who says yes to him [Mary]; and the one who says no to him [Pilate]. Those three names map out the territory in which we all live. Through our lives, we swing towards one pole or the other, towards a deeper yes, or towards a deeper no. In the middle of it all stands the one who makes sense of it all, the one into whose life we must try to grow, who can work with our yes, and can even overcome our no.[1]

This is the compelling figure who stands at the heart of Christianity and came, thankfully, to stand tall at the centre of my own faith.

1 Jesus brought God down to earth

If you are the God of limitless presence, the One who sustains a universe of unimaginable scale, the very ground and rationality of existence itself – then it's going to be hard to make yourself known to those endearing and infuriating specks of stardust called human beings. Men and women need something manageable, something within our own frame of comprehension, something personal. Someone, perhaps? If God were to be understood and be able to make a difference to our lives, there was probably no alternative to God giving himself to us in a human life. Yes, of course it's a paradox, but it's like a performer so entering the genius of a piece of music that he's saturated in the vision and imagination of the composition; he's totally at one with the mind and heart of the composer, and thereby enables others to encounter the music in exactly the way the composer intended, with all the accuracy, passion and love with which he wrote the score.[2] Jesus inhabited his Father's score precisely.

Jesus brings God down to earth. There's no gap between Father and Son. And the incredible thing is that people started speaking of the human Jesus and the everlasting Father in the same breath so soon after Jesus had been seen and known around the fields and lanes of Galilee. In the Acts of the Apostles we find the first martyr, Stephen, commending his spirit to Jesus, not to God. Paul was in no doubt about the exalted role of Jesus Christ – read the first chapter of Colossians and be amazed! It seems that the first followers of Jesus simply couldn't avoid the conclusion that during the ministry of Jesus they had been walking with God. Theologians and ordinary Christians have been trying to work this out ever since.

2 Jesus lived a life of radical, subversive freedom

A wise old bishop used to say: 'Whenever people see me off with a casual "Take care," I want to say to them, "No, no; take risks!"' Our lives can be too circumscribed with caution, anxiety and the fear of freedom. But Jesus would have none of it. He lived on the edge right from the start of his ministry, challenging the heavy-duty interpretations of religion that kept the scribes and Pharisees in business, and taking his listeners on daring journeys of the spirit. He hung out with all kinds of low-life, insulted the religious authorities, advocated a laid-back attitude to the law, and generally encouraged people to get a life. He taught with reckless freedom and refused to compromise even when he finally went into the heart of enemy country in Jerusalem. If I'd been a disciple I think I'd have been saying: 'Jesus, couldn't you just back off a little; maybe turn down the rhetoric? Just a bit more subtlety in your choice of targets? Otherwise this is going to end in disaster.' There's a song in the rock opera *Jesus Christ Superstar* with the discerning title 'Could We Start Again, Please?' But Jesus is flying too high and too fast for his disciples to stop him now.

This radical freedom has long appealed to oppressed peoples (slaves in the Deep South, black people under apartheid), the poor reading their Bibles in the shanty towns of South America, students and young people in fashionable revolt in the West. It also appeals to that part of all of us that would love to live more authentically and with fewer self-imposed constraints. In many people there's a free spirit that believes in a larger world where things are done differently, and Jesus speaks to that proto-rebel. He too would probably say: 'No, no; take risks!'

3 Jesus taught with wonderful immediacy

Jesus was a master of communication. He didn't start with the dusty conventions of religious protocol but with the stuff of life before people's eyes. His key theme was 'the Kingdom of God' now breaking into the life of the world, but to explore what that meant he spoke of farmers sowing fields and casual workers in vineyards, of children who ran off to make their fortune and people who turned down dinner invitations, of crooked magistrates and victims of GBH, of friends who turned up after midnight looking for a bed and people who found treasure buried in a field. It was all so vivid. He was a consummate storyteller and held people spellbound by his style of teaching. Albert Einstein once said: 'As a child I received instruction in the Bible and in the Talmud. I am a Jew, but I am enthralled by the luminous figure of the Nazarene. No one can read the Gospels without feeling the actual presence of Jesus. His personality pulsates in every word.'[3] It was this personality that had thousands of people chasing round the lake to catch up with him and sit at his feet. In him, the message, the style and the personality came together in a perfect synthesis, and at some unnamed level people knew they were being addressed with an authority that could only belong to God.

This authority had extraordinary spin-offs. They're normally called miracles, though whether they were breaking natural laws, or merely speeding them up, or even appealing to a deeper law of reality (love?), is hard to say. The problem for a sceptical age is that the Gospels are heavy with evidence. Whatever else he did, Jesus healed. He seemed to create a space where God could act in freedom and where unpredictable things could occur (not always; it was tough going in his home town). I suppose as quantum physics and chaos theory disclose a universe of ever greater openness, the activity of the God who sustains and suffuses everything shouldn't be a great surprise. The idea of miracle will always be mysterious but it can't be ruled out *a priori*.

4 Jesus practised simplicity and hospitality

When I last moved to a new job we needed one and a half pantechnicons to gather up our possessions from the north of England and proceed slowly down the A1. It was a far cry from the self-drive van we had hired to set up our first home. Part of the freedom of Jesus was the way he could sit light to the preoccupations and obsessions that pull the rest of us out of shape. He's really not bothered about ownership; it's the finding of the last lost object that matters. He's not all that concerned about common-sense justice either; it's more important to make sure that every vineyard labourer gets what his family needs than to assess how long he's worked. He sits loose to home comforts too: foxes have warm holes, and birds have well-padded nests, but Jesus depends on people not sending him packing when he rolls up to tell them about the Kingdom of God (though he seems to have had a few female backers with a bit of money on some occasions – Mark 15.41).

What's more, Jesus is spectacularly free of boundaries. He's the one who won't leave anyone behind. He's never disgusted – never believing that a leper, a prostitute, a woman with gynaecological problems, an epileptic, a soldier from the hated occupying forces, or whoever else, is beyond the circle of his compassion. He never seems to say no. At the deepest level he seems to be hospitable to anyone and everyone. Equally, he'll accept hospitality from anyone – leper (Simon), fraudster (Zacchaeus, Levi), leader of the Pharisees (Luke 14), friend (Mary and Martha), or indeed the unknown supporter who owned the Upper Room. This is a man truly at ease with himself and offering that same ease to those of us who, sadly, have so much less imagination.

5 Jesus died through tragic necessity

Jesus flew too close to the sun; it was bound to end in melted tears. Jesus had come up against so many vested interests. He came to Jerusalem and put it all on the line. 'This is what God is offering – a Kingdom of untold freedom, justice and joy. Here's the truth. What do you make of it?' And they answered: they wanted none of it. Writer Alison Morgan puts it this way:

> The human condition remains the same: we are like flies caught on the sticky threads of an invisible web, trapped by the deathliness of our own worldview. Jesus did not come to fiddle with the web or console those stuck on its threads; he came to

shout at the top of his voice that the spider's power was now broken – that we would know the truth and that the truth would set us free.[4]

But as yet, men and women couldn't believe that brave announcement. They had to destroy that which showed them up so badly.

All you need for a crucifixion is a toxic mix of religious conservatism, economic self-interest and political expediency – and one innocent victim. The cross is a place of tragedy and chaos. We shouldn't try and tidy it up into a neat theory. There are a number of theories around; they can speak for themselves. But the deeper truth is that this cross is a mystery to enter rather than a philosophical problem to solve. What can you say on Good Friday? Not much, really; it's too awful. You just have to keep telling the story.

6 Jesus rose from the dead with grace and power

Now we've hit the intellectual buffers. We might just about cope with a suffering God, but a man, no matter how good, rising from the dead? Pull the other one. And yet we can clearly state that the whole of the Christian faith rests entirely on this one fact. Without this event we would simply have another failed messiah, hung out to dry in the accustomed Roman fashion, with a few hundred disillusioned followers sliding back to their old life with a mixture of regret and graceful sadness. The resurrection is the single, blistering, whirligig event that changed everything.

And somehow the event has to be located in history, the kind that's open to public investigation and scholarly examination. Much could be said (and has been said: N. T. Wright's study has over 800 pages[5]), but at least let's recognize that if there had been an empty tomb but no sightings of Jesus, it would have been assumed that the body had been stolen. Similarly, if there had been various eyewitness sightings of Jesus but no empty tomb, it would have been assumed that these were merely the sad but understandable projections of bereaved followers. Only if both factors – the empty tomb and the sightings – were true together could anyone conclude that Jesus had been raised from the dead. Moreover, something astonishing changed a terrified, demoralized group of young men from the north country who wanted nothing more than to avoid capture and slip back to Galilee first thing on Monday morning, into the world-changing band of brothers who would instead capture the imagination of the Roman Empire and eventually of the whole world. That 'something' needed to be a staggering experience, not just a gradual return of optimism. Resurrection fits the bill.

And yet, of course, the resurrection is still an event that remains ultimately mysterious. As David Ford says in *The Shape of Living*: 'There is no ready-made worldview into which it fits . . . if we think we have a framework that contains it, then we have not grasped the sort of event it is.'[6] What we are left with, however, is an event that still ricochets around the world, bringing untold delight and hope to millions.

7 Jesus left behind thrilled, but still uncertain, followers

A notice in an Austrian ski lodge said: 'Not to perambulate the corridors in the hours of repose in the boots of ascension.' That well-meaning instruction has something of the same opacity as the Ascension itself. I once saw a performance by the Reduced Shakespeare Company of *The Bible: The Complete Word of God (abridged)*. It was full of wonderful, affectionate humour, but when they came to the cross, resurrection and Ascension, they told it straight. An actor simply stood on stage and said: 'And then Jesus ascended into heaven and sat at the right hand of the Father. And he will come again in glory to judge both the living and the dead, and his kingdom will have no end.' There was a pause, and then he said: 'That's pretty cool.' And then the humour went on.

The Ascension is indeed pretty cool, but we're not likely to be able to describe it very well. Whatever happened in time and space, it became clear to the apostles that Jesus was bringing to an end the month or so of sporadic sightings and conversations, the period that Chris Russell describes well as the future 'grazing' against the present.[7] The spatial imagery of going 'up' is simply a conventional way of describing the true destiny of the risen Christ. But in leaving the disciples' immediate presence, it could be said that Jesus took humanity to the right hand of God. No longer can we say, 'I'm only human,' because in the ascended Christ we become more truly human than ever, and indeed, therefore, most like God. Bringing that theology back down to earth, the disciples were still not certain what to do with their joyful confidence. Jesus had told them to wait to 'receive power', so they went back to their upper room in Jerusalem; but apart from replacing the now deceased Judas and worshipping in the Temple, they were still left wondering what to do next. Little did they know.

8 The Spirit of Jesus fell on his followers

It was an ordinary morning. They were clearing away the breakfast things and sorting out the day's jobs. The upper room where they'd spent so much time recently was suffering from an excess of male neglect. But then, as from nowhere, came a communal experience of such overwhelming energy and power it seemed as if a gale was blowing through the room and flames of fire were dancing around the disciples. The events of this extraordinary morning are described in Acts 2. What a movie camera would have picked up I've no idea, but the effects of that morning are still being felt today. The disciples were practically thrown out into the world. Never again were they unsure what their task was. The Spirit drove them out to tell the good news of God's unlimited generosity to the whole unsuspecting world. The steam generated in that upper room was converted into power, because the test of this experience wasn't their wonderful feelings but their effective witness.

This kind of experience isn't just locked in the past. God's Spirit blows with reckless freedom through his weary world. John McCarthy was held prisoner for five years in Beirut and it drove him mentally and emotionally to a very dark place, but down there in the pit he had a life-saving experience:

> One morning my fears became unbearable. I stood in the cell sinking into despair. I was on my knees, gasping for air, drowning in hopelessness and helplessness. I thought I was passing out. I could only think of one thing to say – 'Help me please, oh God, help me.' The next instant I was standing up, surrounded by a warm bright light. I was dancing, full of joy. In the space of a minute, despair had vanished, replaced by boundless optimism. What had happened? I had never had any great faith, despite a Church of England upbringing. But I felt I had to give thanks. But to what? Unsure of the nature of the experience, I felt most comfortable acknowledging the Good Spirit which seemed to have rescued me. It gave me strength to carry on and, more importantly, a huge renewal of hope – I was going to survive.[8]

The Holy Spirit goes by many names – she isn't proud. She's unpredictable, untidy, unconventional and truly wonderful. And without her we can't live and thrive as Christians but only take a long time to fade away.

9 Jesus Christ relates to the Father and the Holy Spirit in the Trinity

You'd probably rather not go into this in detail. It took the early Church many centuries and many furious arguments to end up with the conviction that God is three 'persons' in one God, 'the glory equal, the majesty co-eternal'. For a wonderfully entertaining (and accurate) statement of Trinitarian belief, look up the Athanasian Creed on Wikipedia. If you thought string theory was complex . . . However, the essence of the Trinity is that the three 'persons' are a community of mutual love and encouragement, expressing the dynamic joy at the heart of God. Christians don't believe in three Gods, nor that any one person of the Trinity is superior to any other. Rather, the Trinity is a way of doing justice to the experience of Christians that they encounter God in different ways – in the creative love of the Father, the saving friendship of the Son, and the sustaining energy of the Spirit. Perhaps the best way of understanding what Christians believe on this is to spend time before Rublev's famous icon of the Trinity. And then to pray.

10 Jesus will 'return' and gather all things into himself

Here we're up against the limitations of language and the regrettable detail that we are not God. The New Testament poetry of 'a new heaven and a new earth' (Rev. 21.1), of God gathering up all things in Christ, 'things in heaven and things on earth' (Eph. 1.10), and the new Jerusalem 'coming down out of heaven from God' (Rev. 21.2) – all these are beautiful but forlorn attempts to foresee the unforeseeable. Cosmologists tell us that the universe will probably come to an end in either the Big Crunch or the Big Freeze, depending on whether the universe collapses in on itself or expands until it cools to a state of frozen entropy. Either way, the alternative poetic language of religion sees all this as being within the purposes of God, as the new creation bursts through the old, and Christ is revealed as both Lord and logos – the divine principle of creation – and the Kingdom of God is complete. So God will be all in all (1 Cor. 15.28). Fortunately, this is beyond our comprehension, and quite a long time off . . .

Quote: From Bono, lead singer of Irish rock band U2

Bono was asked if the idea of Jesus being Son of God wasn't far-fetched. He said: 'No, it's not far-fetched to me. Look, the secular response to the Christ story always goes like this: He was a great prophet, obviously a very interesting guy, had a lot to say along the lines of other great prophets, be they Elijah, Muhammad, Buddha or Confucius. But actually Christ doesn't allow you that. He doesn't let you off that hook. Christ says, No, I'm not saying I'm a teacher, don't call me a teacher. I'm not saying I'm a prophet. I'm saying: "I'm the Messiah." I'm saying: "I am God incarnate." And people say: No, no, please, just be a prophet. A prophet we can take. You're a bit eccentric. We've had John the Baptist eating locusts and wild honey, we can handle that. But don't mention the "M" word. Because, you know, we're gonna have to crucify you.'[9]

Taking it further

The ten key points here take us through the life, death and new life of Jesus. What are the ten key things about Jesus that attract you to him? Or what are your favourite ten stories about his life, and why? Or what ten questions would you most like to ask him?

9

Ten reasons why Christianity is so long lasting

Given the hostility that Christianity attracts in Western culture today it might be a surprise that the number of Christians worldwide is growing at such an extraordinary rate. There are many who think that Christianity ought to be in terminal decline rather than in jaunty good health. Meanwhile, Western culture races around, dazed by its own success, but lacking direction and depth. That wise monk Thomas Merton once observed that many people seem to spend their whole life climbing the ladder of success only to find, when they get to the top, that the ladder is leaning against the wrong wall. And there at ground level, patiently getting on with the job, is that old-fashioned Christian religion the West is supposed to have grown out of. It's very perplexing. So why is Christianity so long lasting?

1 Christianity is about a person, not a theory

This faith doesn't point to a set of ideas; it points to the person of Jesus Christ. Christianity is scandalously particular about its focus. There's no obfuscation or wandering off into vague platitudes, nor any foolproof system for self-improvement or sanctity. There's a human life, historically located and minimally recorded; a life of unequalled wisdom and com-passion, a life that ended on a gallows but rose again in a garden, a first-century, provincial Hebrew life. But everything we need is packed into that life. It's either madness on the part of God or genius. But one thing is certain; you can't duck the central figure. Equally, you can't pick and choose from a menu of Great Thoughts. You have to deal with a human life and the dexterity with which Jesus handled every human situation. You're faced not with theories but with character, and the character of Jesus challenges every onlooker and would-be disciple. As for me, I can't get him out of my system.

2 Christianity affirms the depth and value of every human life

A priest bent over to talk to an elderly lady in a nursing home and said gently: 'Do you know who I am?' 'No dear,' said the lady, 'but if you ask Matron, I'm sure she'll tell you.' Who we are, and what value we have, are ultimate existential questions. There are no 'ordinary people' in a Christian vision of humankind. There's glory in everyone because we are all, priest and elderly lady alike, made in the image and likeness of God. That last phrase shouldn't be trotted out lightly. If we are made in the image and likeness of God we must be of infinite value to God and to each other. A rabbi taught his disciples that they must have two pockets in their clothes so that they could reach into each pocket as necessary. In one pocket would be a piece of paper with the words: 'For my sake was the world made.' In the other pocket would be a scrap of paper with the words: 'I am dust and ashes.' Both are true, but if we are dust, we are dust that dreams. We have a destiny far beyond the mundane. This translates in Christian action into a cascade of concern for justice, compassion, pastoral care and the reordering of society. There is in the Christian storeroom a kindness beyond limits which stems from valuing the depth, detail and richness of every human life made, incredibly, in the image of God.

3 Christianity has a wonderful model of God

'Three in one, one in three, perfectly straightforward. Any doubts about that, see your maths master.' So said the schoolmaster in Alan Bennett's play *Forty Years On*. But it's undeniable that some people glaze over when others start talking about the Trinity as three Persons in one God. But this model is quite brilliant. It reflects the experience of the first Christians that they knew God in creation (the Father), in history (the Son), and in themselves (the Spirit). God above, God beside, God within. God to protect, to befriend, to inspire. There is a completeness in this understanding of God that is both simple and complex, accessible and subtle. It asserts the rich, dynamic relationships that exist in God and puts on record that God is a community, forever dancing to the melody of love. Much theology springs from this source. If you're in doubt as to how to sound intelligent in a Christian discussion, my advice is to always say something about the Trinity . . .

4 Christianity is realistic about evil

Mark Twain once sent a telegram to a dozen of his friends saying: 'Flee at once – all is discovered.' They all left town immediately. They didn't know what had been discovered, but they all knew that there were things that could be discovered about themselves that they'd rather not be known. When the incessant noise of self-promotion and fake confidence has died away, we're all too aware of our failings. There's a fatal flaw which runs through life, a fracture at the heart of things which emerges in different forms in different places – a tsunami, a massacre, a cancer, a deceit, a theft, a lie. Deep in our hearts we know that life – and our own life in particular – is not as it was meant to be. In the silence we're deeply uncomfortable with that knowledge, but as we have no way of handling the pain of this dissonance, we return as quickly as possible to the noisy surface distractions. But we can't change our reality as if we're flicking a remote control; the deep problem remains, and it remains inadequately analysed. The truth is that where the fracture appears in our own lives (and not in the natural world), the core problem is that we invariably try to remove God from his world and ours. We reduce him to a walk-on part. That's the essence of sin, and Christianity doesn't shirk that description.

Western culture tries to soften these dark realities and swap the labels of good and evil, but Christianity will have none of it. The mystic Simone Weil wrote: 'Imaginary evil is romantic and varied; real evil is gloomy, monstrous, barren and boring. Imaginary good is boring; real good is always new, marvellous, intoxicating.'[1] So it is that light and darkness had to come into fatal conflict. It happened, symbolically and historically, on the cross, and although evil seemed to prevail, it was broken in doing so. Christianity is realistic about evil and about the cost of dealing with it. It took the death of God's Son.

The other side of this reality is that the Christian faith allows life to be messy and people to fail. The Bible is stacked high with men and women who failed in human terms at some crucial stage of their lives. So do we, for we share the frailties of all men and women. But God doesn't demand constant success; he's more interested in our direction of travel. Readiness to get up and stagger on is the characteristic he values most.

5 Christianity has a bias to the disadvantaged

A young man in his twenties wrote in a Sunday newspaper about his very disfiguring disease of neurofibromatosis. He said:

> I kind of got used to the bullying, and people staring at me. I almost felt like shouting: Bring it on! C'mon, what have you got? The more people stared, the more I rebelled. I was fighting fire with fire. The only place that didn't happen was at church. I know this is going to sound like a cliché, but when I walked

into the church it was the first time that nobody seemed to care what I looked like. Initially I went there to do a bit more rebelling, but everybody was so warm, friendly and patient with me. I don't go around shouting it from the rooftops, but I'm a Christian.[2]

This is the characteristic Christian 'preferential option' for the disadvantaged. We have this bias for two reasons: first, we're all made in the image of God and deserving of the deepest care, and second, we recognize that every one of us is carrying a heavy load of some kind and it's our privilege to help each other along the road. The biblical story is aflame with concern for the oppressed and disadvantaged, and Jesus in his ministry clearly put the poor and marginalized centre stage; indeed, so much was this the case that he saw himself in each one of them. 'Just as you did it to one of the least of these, who are members of my family, you did it to me' (Matt. 25.40). Jesus doesn't allow us a nice shiny God, vacuum packed for cleanliness, untouched by dirt and death. He points to, and lives as, a suffering God. As the martyred theologian Dietrich Bonhoeffer put it, 'only the suffering God can help'.[3] Christians will always court unpopularity when they speak up for the poor, whether it be over welfare cuts at home or development aid overseas, but that's the authentic voice of Christianity. God is passionate about justice.

6 Christianity affirms the material world and its creativity

It's been said before: matter matters to God because he invented it. The poetry of Genesis makes clear that 'God saw everything that he had made, and indeed, it was very good' (Gen. 1.31). Note this approval applied to 'everything'. The primary nature of all created matter is good; only secondarily did it get corrupted. Moreover, matter provides scaffolding for spirit; without it, spirit would be as shapeless as a body without a skeleton. So Christianity of all the major religions has a very positive stance towards the material world. Religious concerns are not disconnected from everyday life, floating in a warm spiritual bath away from the cares of the world. They're worked out in the world of mortgages, social media, austerity measures and Premiership football. This is not a world to escape from but to be immersed in, just as Jesus was completely engaged in the life of his corner of Palestine in the years of the incarnation. The goals and methods of industry, the banking sector, the media, the law and the scientific community are as much Christian issues as the concerns of the Church for evangelism and pastoral care. It follows that Christianity is also deeply committed to the arts, where over the centuries religious themes have been a major subject of painters, poets, musicians, playwrights and others. Indeed, artists are often much sought after companions, as the Church tries to 'tell all the truth, but tell it slant' (Emily Dickinson). There's nothing curmudgeonly about the Christian world-view. Every activity in God's world is a thing of interest and a potential source of delight.

7 Christianity is a verb before it's a noun

Christianity is something you *do*, but I know my inclination is to *think*. I taught theological students the art of theological reflection for many years and will happily talk endlessly about the theological issues raised by some critical incident or pastoral encounter. But first of all there need to have been the pastoral encounters to reflect on, and they don't happen if you spend all your time sitting and thinking. Christian action is the key distinguishing mark of a vibrant faith. If faith isn't applied and making a difference, then people are entitled to ask why they should be interested in it. One of the joys of ministry is being part of a Church in which the members are giving 22 million hours of voluntary service to the community *outside the church* every month. It's the faith of these good people that lights their blue touchpaper and sets them off. I see them at work in family centres, hospitals, care homes, charities, night shelters, food banks, credit unions, with children, the elderly, drug users, prisoners, indeed wherever there's need for a strong, steady hand. It's a staggering commitment to the common good. And it goes with the territory; it's what being a Christian means.

Part of the energy that propels Christians into these pieces of work is their strange gift of hope. Whatever the darkness, they see the possibilities of light. There's an Eastern proverb that says: 'The candle is a non-conformist. It says to the darkness: "I beg to differ."' Hope quickly moves past the stage of asking who is to blame for the past mess, and asks instead how we can create a better future. It could be called the 'eschatological preference'. But hope sometimes needs strong emotional energy to get lift-off because of the dire situation it faces. St Augustine described that emotional energy like this: 'Hope has two beautiful daughters: anger and courage. Anger at the ways things are, and courage to ensure they don't stay the way they are.' It's what must have inspired Lord Shaftesbury when he championed so much social reform in the nineteenth century, and what made Chad Varah set up the Samaritans when a young girl committed suicide because she didn't know the ways of her body, and what led Jean Vanier to start setting up his L'Arche communities to give dignity to people with learning difficulties. The stories are beyond counting, except in the halls of heaven. Authentic Christianity makes a difference.

8 Christianity offers a radical reassessment of life and death, and power and weakness

The cross and resurrection play havoc with our normal understanding of life and death. Nothing in religion prepares us for the beauty and terror of a crucified God. Nothing in human experience leads us to expect the extraordinary shattering of death that we see in the Easter tomb. The cross stands in solemn warning over against all human pride and arrogance. So much has to be thought through afresh. So much is paradoxical. Death can overcome God, but love will overcome anything. Life is wonderful, but if we try to save it, we'll lose it. If we give everything up, we'll find even more than we had. If we want to lead, we must be the servant of everyone. The first will be last – and the other way round. Everything about power and weakness has to be rethought. When Jesus met Pilate, who had the power and who had the authority? When Desmond Tutu faced De Klerk in apartheid South Africa, who had the power and who had the authority? And so it goes on. That's the fascinating, elusive quality of a faith that at its heart isn't propositional but personal. It depends on a long, patient, curious engagement with this compelling figure of Jesus, called the Christ. And in the process, life and death will never be the same again.

9 Christianity is trans-cultural

Of all the great world religions Christianity is the one that has taken root in every continent and culture. Other religions are more culture-specific. They spread, of course, but they don't become embedded as the Christian faith has done. This isn't a claim to superiority: simply a reason for this faith being so pervasive and long lasting.

10 The core value of Christianity is love

When all other words about God have got tired and fallen by the wayside, the word that best describes God in Christian understanding is that he is Love; Love in its pure, uncut, undiluted form. And Christianity is about the living out of that love, making the character of God real in the life of the world. The word itself is damaged, of course. It hasn't been able to take the weight of expectation laid upon it and has had to settle in our culture for sentiment and fluffy good intentions. The Greeks were more serious about love and made sure it could be understood in four forms: *storge* (affection, as in families), *philia* (friendship, chosen and committed), *eros* (romantic and erotic), *agape* (unconditional, God's distinctive love). Agape is the characteristic Christian form of love of neighbour, reflecting God's love and not seeking any reward. It's the outworking in the world of the nature and character of God, love that is uncalculating, unprotected, unconditional. If we are to believe the Christian understanding of God, this love is what creates and sustains the universe. This is what the grain of the universe is made of, so to go against it is to be afflicted by the splinters we call sin. This is the supreme source of energy that once empowered Jesus and continues to empower his followers. This is the core value of Christianity because it's the core of God's nature. God is love. End of story. Full stop.

Story

The head of the Jesuit Order Fr Arrupe was visiting some Jesuits working in a desperately poor slum in Latin America. During his visit he celebrated Mass for the local people in a decrepit building with cats and dogs wandering in and out freely. This is what he wrote afterwards: 'When it was over a big man whose hang-dog look made me almost afraid said, "Come to my place. I have something to give you." I was undecided, but the priest who was with me said, "Accept, Father, they are good people." I went to his place; his house was a hovel nearly on the point of collapsing. He had me sit down on a rickety old chair. From there I could see the sunset. The big man said to me, "Look, sir, how beautiful it is!" We sat in silence for several minutes. The sun disappeared. The man then said, "I don't know how to thank you for all you have done for us. I have nothing to give you, but I thought you would like to see this sunset. You liked it, didn't you? Good evening." And then he shook my hand.[4]

Taking it further

What do you make of these ten reasons for Christianity to be so long lasting? Which would you agree with and which not? Can you think of others? What would an agnostic or atheist say? And do you think the arguments will stand up over the next period of the world's history?

10

Ten Commandments for today

---•◆•---

A letter to *The Guardian* went like this: 'There's nothing like teenage diaries for putting momentous historical events in perspective. This is my entry for 20 July 1969: "I went to arts centre in yellow cords and blouse. Ian was there but he didn't speak to me. Got poem put in my handbag from someone who's apparently got a crush on me. It's Nicholas I think. UGH. Man landed on the Moon."'[1] Sometimes it's hard to get things in perspective. In somewhat similar vein, we find it hard to get the momentous Ten Commandments in proper perspective. We've become too familiar with them and they've lost their significance. But they have clearly had a huge impact on millions of lives over the centuries. Many a church has them emblazoned on the east wall behind the altar. They've guided and directed countless Sunday school children. They've been the benchmark for many a nation's life. But how do they apply today when we live in the house of the bewildered? Doctor Who says to a crying baby in an episode in the 2011 series: 'Stop crying! You've got a lot to look forward to, you know. A normal human life on earth: mortgage repayments, the nine to five, a persistent nagging sense of spiritual emptiness. Save the tears for later, boyo.'[2] Life is complex. How shall we live our one exciting, precious life? And how can the wisdom of these ancient commandments help us?

1 I am the Lord your God . . . you shall have no other gods before me

Watch what you worship

There are many things that vie for pole position in our ultimate commitments. The list is familiar. Consuming more and more (to less and less effect). Sex with everything (an easy win for advertisers and viewing figures). Ambition to get to the top of the greasy pole (before I meet myself slipping down). Perhaps we don't notice that these have become idols, asking at first, and later demanding, full attention and regular sacrifices. We have to watch what we worship or we'll become the slave of destructive gods which start small but grow into giants. In a society that has forgotten God the spiritual impulse still remains; something has to take on ultimate significance for us. Some of the alternatives are, of course, good in themselves. Chief among these might be the family or a particular social cause or a political ideology. And all may be well – until the expectations placed on an ideal family or a crusading organization prove to be too much, and the idol shatters under the strain. Then we might remember that only God can bear the weight of being divine.

2 You shall not make for yourself an idol

Beware the danger of objects becoming idols

It may not be consumption, sex, ambition, family or a cause that claims our idolatry. It may be a specific object – a car, a house, a wardrobe of clothing, the must-have items of new technology. But it's like drinking saltwater; it just makes you more thirsty, and it distorts your values, the price labels attached to everything in your life. There was great wisdom in the monastic tradition that put poverty as one of the three great vows. Not because being poor has innate virtue but because simplicity of life clears away the urban clutter of material possessions and reminds us that the greatest gifts are being alive and having strong relationships, purpose and dignity. If I was asked what I would pay for my sight I would propose practically everything I own. As it is, I do have my sight, so why am I not more grateful for the amazing free gift I already have? To say that the best things in life are free sounds trite, but it's none the less true. Beware the danger of manufactured objects displacing the astonishing gifts of the Creator.

3 You shall not take the name of the Lord your God in vain

Don't try and enlist God to validate your own ideas

A favourite cartoon of mine has a vicar summing up a discussion at a church council meeting. 'So that's settled then. Jim, Nicola, David, Josh, Diana, Tom and Emily are opposed to the idea. God and I are in favour.' It's very tempting to call in a higher authority to support our own pet projects and ideas. But God is God, and not to be reduced to a Weapon of Personal Enforcement. Nor is it acceptable to try and make God the Life President of our own personal belief system. We often dress up personal battles and emotional commitments in the evening dress of theological debate. I'm strongly committed to the ministry of women in all three orders of deacons, priests and bishops, and I recognize my temptation to try and trump all comers with the clear and obvious fifth ace of God's Will. I must not make wrong use of the name of the Lord my God.

4 Remember the Sabbath day, and keep it holy

Live your life in a Godly balance and give God time to refresh you

A week is a long time in politics, banking and discipleship. And at the end of it we're entitled to be weary and to have a day of down-time. But the Sabbath is a principle as well as a day. It's about living in a healthy rhythm of work and leisure, of family, friends and colleagues, of breathing out and breathing in. It's a question of balance. I can hear hollow laughter coming from the next room and feel I ought to retreat at this point. However, pressing on, I know the importance of this balance even if I'm not brilliant at achieving it. Better to have the recognition of failure than to be naive about the damage done by stress, damage done to the emotions, the body, relationships, the future – and to the image of God which we all carry. Above the wreckage of my best intentions the tattered flag of hope still flies. God's unfettered love presses us towards healthy lifestyles in which we can flourish at every level and enjoy the grace of a rounded existence.

5 Honour your father and your mother

Pay special attention to your parents and family

I was born at a very young age and am especially grateful to my parents for thinking of me. They gave me a wonderfully secure base for life. They weren't overindulgent with their two boys (they couldn't be on a vicar's stipend) and they didn't over-fuss. But they loved us and supported us to the hilt. So it wasn't difficult to honour them and give them special attention and love in return. Many people have a much more challenging relationship to work out, for reasons as diverse as the vagaries of human families and personalities, as well as the slings and arrows of outrageous events. But the commandment stands. If it hadn't been for our parents' act of love there would have been no existence for us. In that sense we owe them everything. They may have made mistakes but very few of them would have been malicious; we are all the product of our own upbringing. When parents become old they can be irritating in their conservatism and stubbornness, their ill health and insecurity.

But this is a time to return the commitment they made to us in broken nights when we were small, financial sacrifices when we were growing up, anxiety when we were teenagers, and support when we had finally set sail. Our parents and family aren't chosen, it's true, but they are the special gifts God has given us, and are therefore a unique opportunity to love. And it's worth remembering that we in turn will grow old and unreasonable at some stage.

6 You shall not murder

Don't damage other people by your words or actions

Not many of us will commit murder in our lifetimes, but by the standard Jesus set in the Sermon on the Mount we're not in the clear. 'If you are angry with your brother or sister you will be liable to judgement' (Matt. 5.22). If that's the benchmark and we think back over the last week we may well be in trouble. But the still deeper issue is that of causing damage to others by what we say or do, and there the floodgates can open. When we allow ourselves to join in the criticism of a colleague, when we use our position to put someone down, when we speak sarcastically to a partner or lose our temper with a child – what are we doing but damaging them? Nearly everyone we meet is carrying a burden and a harsh word or a bad decision can put them back years. The golden rule that we should do to other people what we hope they would do to us is a splendid touchstone. Think it through in relation to anyone with whom you struggle to get on. If we extend this commandment further we can see that it means we shouldn't let others, our government or the international community, cause hurt in our name either. The huge protests about Britain's involvement in Iraq or the sustained campaigns about world poverty and climate change are examples of this commandment being worked out by many. The message is clear: Don't damage other people in my name.

7 *You shall not commit adultery*

Be loyal to your partner throughout life

The heart of this commandment for today is to have our sexuality guided by love, and to have our physical relationships truthfully express the level of personal commitment we have with the other person. If we have made a full and final commitment to that other person then that's the context for sexual expression, and we can only make that kind of absolute commitment, by definition, in one relationship. If we try to make that kind of commitment to more than one person, it's false; it can't be 'full and final' but only 'partial and penultimate'. Many people find that understanding of the place of sexuality unbelievable today because they've been brought up in a culture that sees sex in more functional terms simply as an instrument of pleasure. The pursuit of sex can then become a game, played as a kind of erotic Xbox without rules. But when sex isn't guided by love and commitment it becomes selfish and diminishing for all concerned.

Our sexuality is to be celebrated. It's a crucial part of our make-up. But because it's so powerful a force it needs to be embraced by an even more fundamental element of our lives – the need to give and receive love within a framework of loyalty and trust. We live in a society where many of us slip below this bar of loyalty because all of us are vulnerable in the arenas of our lives that are most precious and profound. Married people aren't immune from falling in love with someone who isn't their life partner. We need therefore to hold out to others (and to ourselves) another deep religious instinct as well as commitment, that of forgiveness and understanding. The basic principle of this seventh commandment is that disloyal or selfish use of our sexuality is not God's way for men and women, and that love and loyalty to our partner is always the better way that leads to joy.

8 *You shall not steal*

Don't take what isn't yours, and don't keep what you should be giving away

At the age of 11 I set out on my first shoplifting expedition. A friend more experienced in these matters decided we should go to a neighbouring town and relieve the now deceased Woolworth's of its profit margin. We agreed to split up and regroup in 20 minutes to see what we'd got. I remember standing with a selection of pens, notebooks and pencil sharpeners in my hands and thinking: 'This is it. In my pocket and walk away – or put them back on the shelves. My decision. But it will have consequences.' I put them back. My criminal career collapsed at first base. However, my decision could have gone the other way and who knows where that would have led? My early failure (or success) is a far cry from the millions that are now obtained by fraud or siphoned off in corrupt contracts, but every criminal career starts somewhere. And the principle is the same – we shouldn't take what isn't ours. When our house in Durham was burgled, and when, on another occasion, my credit cards were stolen and well used, I remember feeling outraged less at my financial loss than at the deep unfairness of someone taking what, quite simply, didn't belong to them. It was more than an affront to morality; it was a kink in the right ordering of life. Call me old-fashioned, but it was *wrong*.

There's another side to this issue. As well as not taking what isn't mine, I have another duty not to keep what I should be giving away. Everything I have is a gift – absolutely everything. To have worked for something is only to have a penultimate claim on it. My ability to enjoy the sun now pouring through my window, the comfort of relaxed clothing, the occasional sniffy visits from our slightly superior cat, the computer on which I'm tapping these thoughts – none of this is mine by right, because life and the good fortune I have in being born when and where I was, is all gift. So if I can afford to share my good fortune (and all of us reading this can afford something) then I have a duty to spread the gifts around. People of faith have always understood this, and the money they give to charities is enormous and its scale little known by the rest of society. It's the message we repeat so often to our children when small: 'Give – don't take.'

9 You shall not bear false witness against your neighbour

Don't lie to get yourself out of trouble or someone else into it

Some of the most tragic situations you read about in the press are of people who've been in prison for years for crimes they didn't commit. Often they are there because someone has lied about them to get out of trouble themselves or to work out a grudge. The sense of injustice if you are the person denied your liberty for years, knowing you're innocent, must be one of the hardest human experiences to bear. But at a different level, the temptation to lesser falsities is often before us. You see it in nurseries: 'Tom, did you hit Clare?' 'No, George did it.' (George, meanwhile, is speechless, which makes him look all the more guilty.) In the Senior Management Team they're discussing last month's disappointing figures. 'I'm afraid Sam isn't pulling his weight at the moment,' says his boss, covering up his own mistake when he took his eye off the ball. And so on. Lying can have small beginnings but become a way of life – as we've seen when some rogue trader has lost his firm millions and taken it to the edge of insolvency. Lying at home to get out of an embarrassment is a very effective training ground for a long-term career in lying. Best to stand tall, look your mistake in the eye and admit it. 'Yes, I did hit Clare.' (She was being particularly annoying, of course.)

10 You shall not covet

Live with what you have rather than comparing yourself with others

One of the problems of a consumer mindset is that it isn't based on any absolute limit but is largely controlled by comparisons. We haven't got *as much as* our friends. That new car on the drive opposite is just what I'd like to have. I know we're going to Majorca, but David and Isobel are off to the Maldives – again! Coveting our friends' greater wealth or good fortune creates an insatiable desire for more, and more of more. And insatiable is the key word. We can throw more cars, holidays, gadgets and gizmos into the jaws of envy but the appetite is never satisfied, and we end up suffering material fatigue. By contrast, there's a regular stream of good news stories as people downsize or de-clutter and move out of the rat race to discover a more human scale of life. To live without envy is to find inner freedom. And this principle applies not just to material things. The tenth commandment mentions not coveting your neighbour's wife or slave as well as his ox or donkey. Ox or donkey corresponds well to the new car, and slave might correspond to a home help, but what about coveting the more glamorous wife next door? Back to the seventh commandment. Instead, the deeper wisdom rests with the simple advice: live with what you have; value, enjoy and make the most of the simplest, deep-down gifts, and life will probably blossom in rich and fruitful ways.

Story

The gods had grown tired of the way that mortals constantly messed things up. So they sent out their servants to gather together all the great wisdom of the world and put it into a huge library that mortals could use to learn how to live properly. When the task was completed the colossal library stood proudly in one of the great capitals of the world. However, the library was just too large and intimidating for anyone to want to go in and use it. So the gods sent their servants off again to compress all the wisdom in the library into a single, encyclopaedic volume. When the work was completed the book was widely circulated, but it was too big and heavy. People could hardly lift it, let alone read and use it. Once more the gods sent their servants off to produce, this time, a leaflet with a précis of all the essential wisdom people needed to live and act well, but the people were lazy and many of them couldn't even read. So the leaflet was finally refined into a single word. And the word was sent out on the lips of one special messenger.

And the word?

It was 'love'.

Taking it further

What do you think of the above rephrasing and re-application of the Ten Commandments? How would you have re-presented them? If you could write another ten in addition, which have special relevance for today, what would they be?

11

Ten clichés to avoid

I'm grateful to Christian Piatt for two articles in the *Church Times* which suggested this particular list.[1] We live in a sound-bite culture, but it has to be admitted that Christians have been as guilty as any of trivializing deep and mysterious events by sticking a cliché over them. Sometimes it's a defensive reaction to close down a painful situation. At other times it's a replay of bad teaching they've received from their church. At no time, however, is it wise, because the pastoral damage can be immense.

1 'There but for the grace of God go I'

This is an understandable reaction based on relief and a desire to stand alongside the one who is suffering. The intended message is, 'I'm no better than you; it could have been me.' Unfortunately, the effect is completely the opposite, because the suggestion is that I am somehow favoured and protected from the bad event, whereas the person concerned has been left outside God's grace. God has chosen me and not you. The idea that God has favourites is completely contrary to the example of Jesus who picked up anybody and everybody to receive mercy, the only criterion being their need. The difficult experience someone has suffered is more likely to be the result of bad luck. That sounds like cheap theology, but in fact it's a more profound understanding of suffering (see p. 93, 'God is in control').

2 'Everything happens for a reason'

Try saying that to a victim of rape, torture or abuse. If God is meant to be the reason for that happening then this trite phrase is likely to put the person off God for life. You can see the good intentions of the speaker in trying to find meaning in the midst of tragedy, but this phrase misfires badly. There is indeed deep purpose written into the grain of the universe and everything in it, but that purpose creates a framework for freely acting natural phenomena and human actions (though of course, God is always present within all processes and working for good). To impute purpose to a particular catastrophic event is tantamount to accusing God of cruelty, sadism and evil. Rather, we are always in God's hands, never abandoned and unloved.

3 'God is in control'

Again, how does that sound to the victims of the Asian tsunami or the 9/11 attack on the Twin Towers or a suicide bomber in Iraq? If God is in control, he's making a pretty bad job of it. It's comforting to imagine that the way God interacts with his world is as a kindly father overseeing our lives, but the agonies of human history soon make this easy picture impossible. God doesn't *control* the universe; he *energizes* it. But in the continuous act of creation he creates space for that most precious gift of freedom, with all the dangers and risks attached. Love will always take that risk; it will always limit itself in order to give the recipient dignity. Take a couple who have a baby. In the act of procreation they've ceased to have a 'theoretical' child and now have a particular child; they can no longer 'control' the theoretical child because they have an all-crying, all-waking actual child to deal with. As the child grows older they relate to it not by iron control and rigid discipline but by love, persuasion, reasoning, invitation (and maybe a little bribery). Similarly, in the act of creation God limits his freedom in the interests of love. The philosopher John Macmurray puts it well. He says that the maxim of illusory religion declares: 'Fear not; trust in God and he will see that none of these things you fear will happen to you.' But the maxim of real religion says: 'Fear not; the things you are afraid of are quite likely to happen to you [equals 'may well happen to you'] – but they are nothing to be afraid of.'[2]

4 'The Bible clearly states . . .'

This is a very dangerous phrase. It's usually produced as a knock-down argument when the going has got tough. And as all orthodox Christians regard the Bible as inspired and authoritative, it catches people on the back foot. (They usually don't know their Bibles as well as the one who's sent the missile, either.) The trouble is, this phrase wouldn't be necessary if the issue really was clear. All readings of the Bible are interpretations based on historical and geographical context, type of church and theological background, critical tools, personal experience and a host of other factors. And it has to be said that all of us are selective in our reading of Scripture – not many of us refuse to wear blended fibres or eat shellfish. It's better to start with the presumption that the Bible is the inspired (but not dictated) Word of God, and that the true Word of God to which it points is Jesus. Jesus is the best 'hermeneutical principle' for reading the Bible well, so we need to be in constant conversation with this God-breathed text, reading it through the filter of Jesus Christ.

5 'God called him home'

I do hope this phrase isn't used any more but I rather fear it is. Again, it's meant well. The speaker hopes to reassure the bereaved person that this was a loving father calling a loved one to eternal bliss, like a caring parent calling a child in for tea at the end of the afternoon. But again, what idea of God lies behind this apparently innocent saying? Here is a God who decides, 'Right, I think I'll have that one today; oh yes, and that one and those two . . .' If this is how God works, I wish he'd taken Hitler in 1933 rather than my young sister-in-law who died of leukaemia. It's an intolerable image of a casual, arbitrary God. The God disclosed by Jesus longs for the well-being of all his children, and went to the furthest reaches of darkness to overcome all that stands in our way. God welcomes us home, certainly; but calls us intentionally? No.

6 'If only we could live like they did in the early Church'

There's an attractive sentimentality about this phrase. We see the early days of the Church as exciting and daring, with regular miracles and a common life in which everybody got on with everybody else and shared their possessions and gave money to the needy, and the general population thought they were marvellous (Acts 2.43–47). If this is how it was, the golden period was soon over. Many Christians were dispersed in the persecution following the killing of Stephen; then, as new churches were set up, it's clear from Paul's letters that they all had real problems – of relationship, of theology, of how to worship, of how to deal with troublemakers and so on. In fact we never meet a church in the New Testament that didn't have problems. The truth is that churches have always been made up of fallible people, and each community is asked to address its issues with the grace, mercy and peace we see in Jesus. We have to face our own reality rather than yearning for a mirage. There are some lovely ideas in the picture of the early Church that we get in Acts, but it's not a blueprint.

7 'We've always done it this way'

I suppose most people are sufficiently aware of this sad phrase not to use it in its pure form. But there are a hundred variations, and they all point to a lack of faith. It may be that the particular practice doesn't need changing, but not to look at it on the spurious grounds that 'we've always done it this way' is to deny that God is an expert in new creation, resurrection and renewal. W. H. Auden said, 'We would rather be ruined than changed,' and some psychologists reckon that most of us can't change more than 5 per cent of our received wisdom at any one time. So managing change is an art of supreme emotional intelligence. But Christians of all people ought to be open to change. Our faith is based on an event that threw the gears of creation into reverse, and millions of people have been profoundly changed by this glorious good news. So to label, box and bury any religious practice on the grounds that we've always done it this way and over my dead body will it change, is tragically short-sighted.

8 'If we have enough faith . . .'

'If we have enough faith . . .' this person will be healed, or the money for the church extension will be raised. We've probably all heard it, and maybe even said it in one form or another. It's quite understandable as a call to serious prayer but it has a number of dangers. The theology behind this phrase suggests that if we believe and pray hard enough, God will be persuaded. If we build up a sufficient volume of prayer God will give in and say, 'All right then; you win.' I've done my share of asking congregations to pray for particular projects and I marvel at what the people of God raise for things they believe in, but God doesn't have to have his arm bent behind his back. God is always on our side – that's the first rule of intercession. He too longs for the well-being of the person for whom we're praying. God doesn't need persuading. What he needs is enough of us to catch a clear vision and align ourselves with God's purposes (which may or may not include our pet project) and with his active love (which may or may not be able to heal the person we're praying for). Prayer clarifies our hearts and minds, in something like the way that time gives a jug of water from a pond the opportunity for the detritus to settle. Then, when all is clear, wallets tend to open for the church extension, and we know what to do for the person who is ill.

9 'We pray, Lord, that you would just . . .'

OK, this is a personal grumble but it's annoying. 'That you would just . . .' do this, that or the other is a lazy cliché, part of the irritating language of Zion that puts off the outsider not versed in these codes. I appreciate that all human groups, from families and darts teams to lawyers and rugby commentators, design their own languages, but we have the privilege of being able to talk with God 'as with a friend' (Exod. 33.11). Would we say to a friend, 'I ask that you would just pass me the salad'? It would be good if our language could be natural and honest and so not irritate grumpy old Christians like me.

10 'Let's . . .'

Here's another personal grouse. Many sermons seem to end with an exhortation to do something new, and it comes out as, 'So let's . . .' The trouble is that this kind of encouragement so easily comes across as yet another demand, another duty to add to my bulging backpack of guilt. We don't come to church for more law; we come for grace. The end of most sermons ought to release us and let us fly. We've been exposed to the gospel that sets prisoners free, prisoners of all kinds, including all of us who live with multiple failures. What we need at the end of a sermon is a power surge of grace. So 'let's' not hear any more 'let's'.

Taking it further

Have you run into many of these phrases, and how did they affect you? Are there other ones you would add to the list? How can we filter them out of our churchy language?

12

Ten ways to pray

The best man was late for the wedding and couldn't find any-
where to park. In desperation he prayed, 'God, I'll go to church
every week for the rest of my life if you'll just find me a park-
ing space.' Suddenly, a space appeared and he shot into it. 'Never
mind, God,' he said, 'I just found one.' Unfortunately, many
people's prayers don't move on much from this strategy of last
resort. And yet the instinct to pray is universal and irrepressible; far more people pray than go to church. But what puts
people off praying more seriously is the fear of failure and the
uncomfortable feeling that prayer is a mysterious technique for
Special People like vicars who've learned the tricks of the trade
and nuns who only stay earthbound by having stones in their
shoes. It seems so difficult to know what actually to *do* in prayer.
But maybe it's easier than we think – at least to begin with. Here
are some ideas:

1 Trust your instincts

One of the problems is that as a culture we've poured water over
the burning bush, and then we wonder why all that remains is
the taste of ashes. We don't trust the numinous, or the instincts
that call us to pray. But think back over a normal day. It's pretty
well bound to have included experiences and episodes that call
out of us feelings of thankfulness, need and sorrow. My first view
of the sea this morning as I drove to the coast, the pleasure
I felt on entering the cottage I've come to in order to write, the
image of my grandchildren that flashed unbidden through my

mind. It's instinctive. So too my desire to do something for two friends with life-threatening conditions; I want to take them somewhere safe and good – and that place seems to be the heart of God. And when I mess up, which I do regularly, I want to take my sorrow and disappointment somewhere big and tough enough to understand and deal with it – and that again seems to be God.

These instincts can be trusted. It's natural to think in the direction of someone/something beyond the here and now, and that's the start of prayer. These thoughts become arrow prayers shot randomly towards God throughout the day. Their immediacy has about it the ring of truth because we're responding to real situations in real time and putting them in God's direction. What we may want to do later is to stretch out those instincts into more intentional and longer lasting times of prayer, to enlarge and enhance the initial instincts. What we've embarked on is what others have called thanksgiving, intercession and confession, but we don't need fancy words. It's prayer.

2 Structured prayer

If we decide we want to take prayer seriously we'll soon find we need some structure. Otherwise we'll flop around, not quite sure where to go and what to do. That's why the acronym ACTS was once so popular; it stands for Adoration, Confession, Thanksgiving and Supplication, and gives a clear framework for prayer (though I've always found it hard to summon up adoration on demand and prefer a simpler TSP – Thank you, Sorry, Please). Another well-trusted route to prayer is through a quiet time with the Bible and some Bible reading notes that not only guide us into understanding the book of books but lead us on to pray about the issues that the day's Bible passage have raised for us.

More structured still, and undertaken by millions of Christians all over the world, is some form of Daily Office of morning and evening prayer. These Offices can be complex or very straightforward, but they have at their heart the steady reading of Scripture, psalms and canticles, together with prayer for the world. This is a constant river of prayer and praise making its majestic way towards God, and we simply get into our coracle and get taken by the current. Our prayer is just a drop of water added to the river, but it's a reassuring thought that the river is going there anyway and will carry us, however unholy we're feeling that day (and that might be quite often).

The prayer for the world and for others, whichever of the above structures we use, allows for a lot of invention. Some people use 'cycles of prayer' from their church. Others compile their own lists, with different categories (family, close friends and colleagues, those in special need, local issues, world crises). I find it's particularly helpful to have photos of family, friends and the clergy I support. Another friend uses a 'mind map' approach, drawing different people and places on a large piece of paper with different coloured pens. My father used Christmas cards, five a day, reckoning that these were the people who were in a special relationship with him and who he particularly cared about. There are many such creative ways to make our intercessions more vivid.

3 Lectio divina *(holy reading)*

Reading the Bible can be undertaken as fast food or a longer intimate meal. *Lectio divina* is a smart phrase for reading the Bible slowly and prayerfully in order to encounter God in the process, rather than rushing past him with a smile and a wave. Typically it works in these four phases:

- *Read* the passage (perhaps start with one of Paul's shorter letters or a psalm or the Sermon on the Mount in Matthew 5—7), and because you're reading slowly, note when a word or phrase hits you. It won't take long. This is the place to pause.

- *Reflect* on this phrase, mulling it over, repeating it, chewing it thoroughly, drawing all the goodness out of it. The image of taste is probably the most accurate. It's a process of unhurried reflection, letting the meaning of the phrase feed the soul.
- *Respond* to the thoughts and feelings that have been welling up inside by praying in whatever way seems appropriate – giving thanks, being sorry or determined to change, hammering something out with God, praying about the future. This may lead into a time of:
- *Rest* when you simply stay with God in the silence of the heart. There's no need to rush. God has all the time in the world – and we have quite a bit of it too.

Then we carry on through the passage for as long as we have time for this particular form of prayer. It can be a rich feast.

4 Ignatian meditation

Another posh phrase. But this way of praying has been life-giving for countless people far beyond the Jesuit community from which it comes. The essence of this form of prayer is that we enter a Bible passage (most commonly a Gospel event) and experience it as a participant observer through the immediacy of the senses. So we let our imagination paint the picture; we see the line of hills over the Sea of Galilee and smell the clean air, we feel the sun hot on our back and watch the characters gather to listen to Jesus, noticing their rough clothes and eager faces. Sight, sound, taste, touch, smell – all the senses can be employed. The process goes like this. We read the story attentively, then close our eyes and run the story through slowly, using those senses, taking in the scene, listening to the tone of Jesus' voice, watching how people respond to him, noticing our own feelings. As the story nears its end we might try and move closer to Jesus and ask him about what has just happened, and tell him what it's done to us. We let the conversation (prayer) run on for as long as it will, before carefully leaving that place and time, and returning to the present. This use of the 'baptized imagination' is too subjective for some, but it's a powerful form of prayer for very many people. I've often felt closer to Jesus in this way than in any other form of prayer, and made many discoveries about a familiar Gospel incident that I've never seen before. Try it.

5 Silence and centring prayer

For some people, and for many at some point on their spiritual journey, words are a distraction because they're increasingly called to silence. In a noisy culture like ours, where we're bombarded with music when we go shopping, where television is awash with overexcited sounds, where pubs, sporting fixtures and parliamentary debates are full of raucous voices raised to excess, the sound of silence is becoming increasingly elusive – and ever more necessary. As years went by and ministry became busier and the demands more relentless I found a deep desire for silence growing within me. A monk had warned some of us years before that unless we spent time each day in silence we would burn out, and I could see that becoming a real danger. In the eye of the storm is a still place, a place of peace beyond the howling winds. That's where the silence of eternity is found and where, in our distracted world, many are finding their home.

Silent prayer has no rules. It's more like entering a special place than doing something or asking for anything. The best way to start is to sit comfortably, alert but relaxed, to breathe steadily, and to drop into the still pond a 'prayer word', such as 'My Lord and my God', 'Come, Holy Spirit', or simply 'Jesus', and let it reverberate around our silence. It centres us. This is a word to drop in as often as feels necessary in order to stay present and attentive. A famous variant on this, much used in the Orthodox churches, is the Jesus Prayer – 'Lord Jesus Christ,

Son of God, have mercy on me, a sinner.' This prayer is the constant daily companion of very large numbers of Eastern Christians and it's becoming very popular here too. In any of these 'centring' forms of prayer we're not looking for results – 'holy feelings' are rare – but rather it's something akin to sunbathing, lying still in the glory of God's presence, even if that presence is usually unfelt. Waiting is a core spiritual discipline in this type of prayer. God is. That's all that matters.

6 *The* examen *(or daily DVD)*

Yet another fancy Jesuit name. Ignatius of Loyola, who founded the Jesuits, required his brothers to use this way of prayer at the end of each day. It's a way of noticing what has gone on in the day, what effect the events had on us, and what God was doing in those times and places. Ignatius had a five-fold process, which you're welcome to try, but I find it unduly complex and prefer a simpler version whereby we first pray for insight and then run through the day attentively, as if watching a DVD of the events. The key move is to be aware of how we felt at different times, whether we were encouraged, anxious, grateful, excited or what. Especially we are to notice what took us 'up' emotionally, and what brought us down. We can then reflect and pray about these feelings and what God was saying to us through them. There may be something going on in our inner world that we hadn't been aware of but which is disclosed through our feelings. Or there may be someone we met who we should pray for, or who delighted us when we met. There may be something we got badly wrong but didn't notice at the time. My simplest version of this process is to cast a spiritual Geiger counter over the day and see when it gets excited; those are the moments that can tell us something important is going on. As ever in the fascinating journey of Christian discipleship, the key requirement is simply to pay attention. God is always present and quietly getting on with the tasks of the Kingdom.

If we recognize what it is that God is doing, we can align ourselves with it. There's no better place to be.

7 All of life as prayer

Some years ago Michel Quoist wrote a book of prayers which was ground-breaking at the time. His vision was of a God for whom nothing was off-limits when it came to prayer, a God who was open all hours and ready for anything. He had a phrase about 'all of life being a prayer', and that phrase stuck with me. It's a Celtic vision too. The Celts had prayers for milking a cow or setting out on a journey or building a cottage – just as Michel Quoist had a prayer over a five-pound note, a barbed-wire fence, a brick and a bald head (useful in my case). To say that all of life might become a prayer could sound like a cop-out, but it probably rings true to extroverts for whom settling down quietly to pray feels unnatural, but offering everything to God as a sign of a life surrendered to him makes a lot of sense. 'Whatever you do, in word or deed, do everything in the name of the Lord Jesus, giving thanks to God the Father through him' (Col. 3.17). That's a prayerful reminder I often use at the start of the day. 'Pray without ceasing,' said St Paul (1 Thess. 5.17). The essential test of our faith isn't the length of our prayers but the depth of our love. And that love is both for individuals, and also love in its social form, which we call justice. All of life, therefore, in every dimension, can be offered to God as part of our relationship with him.

8 Prayer with bells and whistles

That sounds irreverent. What I mean is prayer that uses *other things* as a stimulus. For example, I often use music as a way of entering a time of prayer. It could be the slow movement of Mozart's Clarinet Concerto, a Taizé refrain, or some modern praise song – the effect is to draw me into a greater awareness of God. I often use icons as a way of stilling the mind and focusing the heart. With an icon you look not so much *at* the picture as *through* it to the divine Other who looks at you. I have icons from Jerusalem, the Sinai, Romania and elsewhere, and each one is a unique window into prayer. The simple act of lighting a candle, and using its flickering stability as a point of reference, can hold our wandering hearts during prayer ('I am the light of the world', 'The light shines in the darkness and the darkness has never been able to put it out').

Most religious traditions also recognize the value of praying with the body. This may seem decidedly un-British, but the body is a wonderful barometer of our emotions and desires, and there to be used. Try telling a football fan he can only clap politely when his team scores a winning goal in the dying seconds of the match. Children inhabit their bodies with wonderful freedom. Lovers, too, know how to make their bodies speak in many languages. So it shouldn't be remarkable that people of faith often want to tell of their love, penitence, longing, gratitude or desire through the infinitely expressive vehicle of the body. Most of us will keep such gestures for private use, but there's definite liberation to be found here. Arms can be raised in longing and the desire to be filled. They can be held out from the sides, low, in a gesture of offering. Hands can cover the heart as we remember people who are on our heart, then cupped before us as we ask for grace for their needs, before finally returning to our heart. Hands can cover the face in penitence and then open up to receive forgiveness. The body isn't short of ideas – unless, of course, we censor it.

9 Prayer with others

For some people, prayer with others is much easier than prayer by oneself. There's solidarity and encouragement to be found in praying with others which keeps us on track and somehow raises the stakes. Indeed, solitariness in the Christian life has in some senses to be regarded as a variation on the norm of a corporate life lived in fellowship with others. We are part of a Body (Christ's) rather than a pebble in a box of pebbles. Of course, an extrovert may immediately feel at home in group settings, while an introvert may take more persuading. I remember the feeling of success when I eventually prayed openly in a college group for the first time, and I'm still aware, when praying in a group, of focusing too much on getting the words and sentiments right rather than addressing God from the heart. But there is strength in praying together. Another variation is meeting a couple of others in the early morning and praying together before the working day gets going. As ever, the rule is: pray as you can, not as you can't.

10 The Eucharist

The Eucharist, Holy Communion, the Lord's Supper, the Mass – whatever the name, this way of coming before God is for millions of Christians the primary form of prayer. It encompasses everything: the great acts of God in Christ, the concerns of the faithful, the sacramental meal, the sending out to serve. This is the rhythm of the Christian life – coming with our life in our hands, and going with Christ's life in our hearts; coming with our broken lives, going with his healing life. For huge numbers of people on this planet, this is the most concentrated and transforming encounter they have with God. Theologian Sam Wells tells the story of when he was a vicar on a tough Norwich estate and a group of teenagers broke into the service. They came to the front, looked at the bread and wine, and said, 'Can we have some of that?' Sam said, 'Turn around and look at those people. This is the most important thing in their lives. If you can say that, you can have some. If not, we'll talk at the end of the service.' He was right. For those people on that estate, this was the high point of their week. We can pray privately and often, but it's this Great Prayer that gathers us all together around the altar, and it's this action that best sums up our relationship with God.

Story

A seeker asked a monk, 'Where should I look for spiritual enlighten-ment?'

The monk said, 'Here.'

The seeker said, 'When will it happen?'

'It's happening right now,' said the monk.

'Then why don't I experience it?'

'Because you don't look.'

'So what should I look for?' asked the seeker.

'Nothing,' said the monk. 'Just look.'

'At what?'

'Anything your eyes light upon.'

The seeker was getting perplexed. 'Must I look in a special way?' he asked.

'No,' said the monk, 'the ordinary way will do fine.'

'But don't I always look the ordinary way?'

'No, you don't.'

'Why ever not?' demanded the seeker.

'Because to look you must be here,' said the monk, 'and you're mostly somewhere else.'

The spiritual journey starts with being present, and attending to God, who is always present.

Taking it further

How did you start to pray, and who or what has helped you most on the journey? Which of the ten ways of praying, above, do you use and which would you like to try? How else do you pray? What help would you like to go further and deeper in prayer?

13

Ten sustaining prayers

The beauty of writing a chapter like this is that I'm able to choose what to put in it without any semblance of objective justification. So here are ten prayers that I've personally found to bear the weight of much testing and frequent use. Each of us will have our own favourites; it might be worth compiling your own and keeping them by you. You never know when they'll be needed . . .

1 Collect for the Second Sunday of Epiphany

Almighty God,
in Christ you make all things new:
transform the poverty of our nature by the riches of your
    grace,
and in the renewal of our lives
make known your heavenly glory;
through Jesus Christ our Lord.[1]

2 Inspired by Taizé

Keep us, Lord
in the joy, the simplicity and the compassionate love
of the gospel.
Bless us this day
and those who you have given to our care,
through Jesus Christ our Lord.[2]

3 The Methodist Covenant

I am no longer my own, but yours.
Put me to what you will, rank me with whom you will.
Put me to doing, put me to suffering:
Let me be employed for you, or laid aside for you:
Exalted for you, or brought low for you:
Let me be full, let me be empty:
Let me have all things, let me have nothing:
I freely and wholeheartedly yield all things
to your pleasure and disposal.
And now, glorious and blessed God,
Father, Son and Holy Spirit,
You are mine and I am yours.
So be it.
And the covenant now made on earth,
let it be ratified in heaven.

4 From Africa

Creator God,
give us a heart for simple things:
   love and laughter,
   bread and wine,
   tales and dreams.
Fill our lives
with green and growing hope:
make us a people of justice
whose song is Alleluia
and whose name breathes love.

5 *The General Thanksgiving,*
Book of Common Prayer

Almighty God, Father of all mercies, we thine unworthy servants do give thee most humble and hearty thanks for all thy goodness and loving-kindness to us, and to all men. We bless thee for our creation, preservation, and all the blessings of this life; but above all, for thine inestimable love in the redemption of the world by our Lord Jesus Christ; for the means of grace, and for the hope of glory. And, we beseech thee, give us that due sense of all thy mercies, that our hearts may be unfeignedly thankful, and that we show forth thy praise, not only with our lips, but in our lives; by giving up ourselves to thy service, and by walking before thee in holiness and righteousness all our days; through Jesus Christ our Lord, to whom with thee and the Holy Ghost be all honour and glory, world without end.

6 *From the* New Zealand Prayer Book

O God
it is your will to hold both heaven and earth
in a single peace.
Let the design of your great love
shine on the waste of our wraths and sorrows,
and give peace to your Church,
peace among the nations,
peace in our homes,
and peace in our hearts,
through Jesus Christ our Lord.[3]

7 *A Celtic prayer by David Adam*

You Lord are in this place;
your presence fills it;
your presence is peace.

You Lord are in my life;
your presence fills it;
your presence is peace.

You Lord are in my heart;
your presence fills it;
your presence is peace.[4]

8 By John Henry Newman

O Lord, support us all the day long of this troublous life,
until the shades lengthen, the evening comes,
the busy world is hushed, the fever of life is over,
and our work is done.
Then, Lord, in your mercy
grant us safe lodging, a holy rest, and peace at the last,
through Jesus Christ our Lord.

9 St Patrick's Breastplate

Christ be with me, Christ within me
Christ behind me, Christ before me
Christ beside me, Christ to win me
Christ to comfort and restore me.

Christ beneath me, Christ above me
Christ in quiet, Christ in danger
Christ in hearts of those who love me
Christ in mouth of friend and stranger.

10 From the New Zealand Prayer Book

Lord,
it is night.

The night is for stillness.
    Let us be still in the presence of God.

It is night after a long day.
    What has been done has been done;
    what has not been done has not been done;
    let it be.

The night is dark.
    Let our fears of the darkness of the world and of our own
    lives
    rest in you.

The night is quiet.
    Let the quietness of your peace enfold us,
    all dear to us,
    and all who have no peace.

The night heralds the dawn.
    Let us look expectantly to a new day,
    new joys,
    new possibilities.

In your name we pray.[5]

14

Ten ways to enliven your faith

For centuries Habsburg emperors were buried in a particular church in the heart of Vienna. The protocol for the burial required the pallbearers to knock on the door and beg admission for the dead emperor. When asked who the corpse was, they would recite all his royal titles, and after each one had been given they would be refused entry. Finally they would simply give his Christian name, and at that point they would be admitted. In other words, we all stand before God in the nakedness and simplicity of our own identity and our own faith. No one else's experience of faith, nor a mask of borrowed piety, will do. So, how is it going?

I once saw an advert on the London Underground which said: 'Just because you're breathing doesn't mean you're alive.' So with faith. Just because we go to church and keep turning the handle of faith doesn't mean it hasn't got rusty and hasn't become a real effort. Try this: what colour is your faith, and why? Colours mean different things to us, but for me faith could be yellows and greens (alive and fresh), or dark blue and purple (moody, deep), or red and orange (on fire, wild), or brown and grey (dowdy, unrewarding). The interpretations are up to us, but I doubt we always have a yellow, green and red faith. Moreover, colours fade; sometimes they fade away completely. Then what's to be done?

1 Be expectant when you pray, read the Bible and go to church

Expectancy is easily squeezed out of our faith. We started with the possibility of bumping into God round every corner; now we just hope for the odd cameo performance. Sometimes the trouble lies in the fact that we no longer expect to communicate with anyone much in our prayer, or to be addressed personally by God through our reading of the Bible, or to brush against Jesus when we go to church. We domesticate God and downsize our spiritual ambitions. One answer to all this can be to engage first, second, or third gear (wherever we need to start) and start moving forward again by being *expectant* in our faith. This means expecting to encounter God, and training ourselves to recognize the voice and touch of God when we sit in silence or read the Scriptures or go to the rail to receive communion. It's an attitude of the heart, triggered through the mind. I often realize (eventually, when my dull brain has woken up) that when God has gone quiet it's because I've ceased to expect much of him.

2 Find a soul friend

Do you talk to anyone about God? Maybe we do in a home group, but when do we get to talk about faith, prayer, doubt, joy and struggle in a personal way with all defences down? Everyone who's serious about their faith deserves to have a soul friend with whom they can talk about the spiritual journey, the rocky path, the hard decisions, the splashes of delight, the overwhelming moment that would be an embarrassment to mention in the pub. Maybe 'soul friend' sounds too grand. The point is to have someone in our lives with whom we can talk at depth and without reserve, who we know will hear and respect whatever we have to say. How we recognize who this person might be is a mystery. But it's someone we know, perhaps instinctively, could bear the weight of our trust. It may be one of our friends, who is already the person we go deep with, or it may be that we ask someone who we respect at church if they would mind having this kind of conversation with us every so often. Or the vicar or minister will know where there is a list of 'spiritual directors' we can access. Whatever the origin of this special person, he or she will be able to ask the right questions, clarify the problems, suggest new ways through the forest. In other words – be a gift.

3 Practise the presence of God

This is the famous phrase coined by the seventeenth-century French monk, Brother Lawrence, who worked in the kitchens but found God's presence just as real there as in the chapel. He found he could do anything 'for the love of God', even turn an omelette. 'I possess God as peacefully in the bustle of my kitchen, where sometimes several people are asking me for different things at the same time, as I do upon my knees before the blessed sacrament.'[1] He notes that people try all kinds of techniques by which to learn how to pray and love God, but 'is it not a shorter and more direct way to do everything for the love of God, to make use of all the tasks one's lot in life demands to show him that love, and to maintain his presence within us by the communion of our heart with his?' It's all a matter of practising the presence of God.

In our terms this may involve simply remembering with pleasure that God is always with us, here, now, wherever that is. It involves arrow prayers, glancing towards the God who is there. It involves turning the heart easily and regularly towards the God of love. It involves gazing for a moment at the God who holds us in his gaze. Simple? No, but it gets easier with practice. And that's the secret – practice makes progress (not perfect). And God will always be there, awaiting our slow arrival.

4 Go on pilgrimage

I used to live in a house in Canterbury where the pilgrims of ancient times would have gone through our garden to the cellarer's hall, which was the place of welcome. I used to imagine Chaucer watching the Miller, the Plowman, the Summoner and the Wife of Bath making their way into the sacred spaces of the cathedral. One afternoon I met a man in the cloisters who wanted to tell me that this special place had once saved his life when he'd come to the end of his hopes. It was a brief and burning tale.

There's something quite fundamental to human well-being about going to a place that's special to you – it could be quite nearby, or it could be one of the famous pilgrim places, like Jerusalem or Rome, Lindisfarne or Iona. It may require a bit of planning, but the rewards will far outweigh the effort. Pilgrimage jolts us out of our conventional patterns of life and the unrewarding spiritual practices that we may have hung on to. It has the capacity to put us off balance and therefore to make us more open to God, who's always seeking new ways to arrive in our lives. I would recommend pilgrimage to anyone who's lost his way or who's sat down at the side of the path, tired and not at peace.

5 Read three Christian books a year

That sounds rather prescriptive (what's wrong with four books, or 14?), but I've been alarmed to discover that only one in ten churchgoing Christians reads Christian books. If people want to learn about computers or family history or wine or the First World War, they'll read books and magazines to learn more and become more proficient. So why not read about the most important issues men and women face, the issues of life and death, ecstasy and tragedy, love and prayer, the way out of darkness and the way to the stars – the things that faith addresses? It's a joy to watch the light-bulb moments as Christians discover more about their faith, whether they've been reading about who wrote the Bible and why, about the struggles of the early Church to make sense of belief, about how people have understood Holy Communion, about how faith applies to contemporary ethical issues, about how to enjoy prayer, about famous Christians with their stories and struggles, and so on. As someone who writes books, I'd love to see more people reading them! (I covet the line: 'He wrote books that were so little read as to be almost confidential.') But as a Christian with some responsibility for the health of the Church, I'd love more people to experience the fascination and freedom of engaging with Christian thinking. It doesn't have to be heavy; there are books at every level. Three books a year, one a term, to become a more informed and energized believer – it must be a good idea.

6 Do something for others that takes you slightly out of your depth

Faith can become mundane when it's underemployed, just as muscles can become weak when they're unused during a stay in hospital. The philosopher Kierkegaard once wrote of 'a religion about as genuine as tea made from a bit of paper which once lay in a drawer beside another bit of paper which had once been used to wrap up a few dried tea leaves from which tea had already been made twice'.[2] This charming description could apply to a faith which simply isn't being used.

To use a Christian faith is to put it to work in the loving service of others. That's what it's for – to change people's worlds. Faith becomes attractive when it's seen to make a difference, and Christians feel alive in their faith when they see that change happening. I used to take groups of teenagers from Somerset to help run a children's project in inner-city Birmingham during the summer holidays. You could see the teenagers glow with pleasure as they made the multiple adjustments necessary, and some would say afterwards that this was a major turning point in their lives. That experience of having faith turned into action and finding it transformative could be multiplied a million times. If we've run into the sands in our faith, one way to revive it is to turn outwards and to do something risky for others. Seeing God at work outwardly and feeling God at work inwardly is a revitalizing experience, and there's no shortage of places where we could feel suitably out of our depth, whether it be mentoring young people in a challenging school, being a street pastor on a lively Saturday night, volunteering with a night shelter, helping at a lunch club, a credit union or a food bank – or in my case, joining a choir!

7 Go to a different service once a month

Churchgoing can become stale. We know what's going to happen, how the vicar is going to introduce the service, what speed the organ will be played at, when the children will come and go, which of the vicar's six sermons we're going to hear, and so on. As the service has become routinized, so the same may happen to our faith. We no longer expect the gates of heaven to be flung open at 10.30 on a Sunday morning; instead we expect a predictable service, a mediocre sermon and a temperamental heating system. It can be refreshing, therefore, to change the service we go to once a month. If we go to the main morning service, how about a quiet early communion? Or what about that Taizé service you see on the news-sheet but have never tried? Perhaps even go to an evening service in a different church with a contrasting tradition, and see if God can blow away the cobwebs. One of the benefits of being a bishop is that you get to go to so many churches and see how very differently they do things. The downside is that it's the same preacher every time.

8 Start a journal

I have a beautiful book with a superb cover from the Lindau Gospels. There's a catch with a small magnet, which allows the book to close with a satisfying clunk. Inside, when I bought it, were 100 pages of absolutely blank paper. It's my journal. In it I write my thoughts, feelings, intentions, indecisions, reflections, ponderings, at key moments in the year, such as times of transition or stress or when I'm on retreat or have a Quiet Day. It's many things to me. It's a record of a journey, a friend for my innermost life, a joyful reminder of good days and a holding place for bad ones. It's a safety valve and a mirror, a trusty confidant and a merciful companion. It should never be read by others. I know people who use their journal more often than me, some every day. I know other people who think it sounds like a good idea, but have never got round to it. I commend journalling as a helpful way of reflecting on the deepest things in our lives and a good way of capturing our mood and straightening out our thinking. It can be a launch pad for new spiritual directions. And, of course, months later it makes fascinating reading . . .

9 Read the Gospel of Mark in one sitting

And then go through it slowly with Tom Wright's helpful book *Mark for Everyone*.[3] Mark's Gospel was the first to be written and it has the vivacity and immediacy of an eye witness wanting to introduce us to the Life that changed the world. Mark can be read in little more than an hour and it has the freshness and power that makes all but the most jaded mind sit up and take note. We get so used to hearing the Gospel in bite-sized chunks that we easily miss the dramatic sweep of the story. Reading the Gospel in one go has brought many people to faith and it can revive ours. Tom Wright's *For Everyone* series of Bible commentaries is just what it says, and everyone can benefit from a more leisurely journey through the Gospel with this trusted companion. As we read Mark's Gospel the commanding figure of Jesus is almost guaranteed to step out of the thin pages of the Bible and into our lives.

10 Be intentional about growing in faith

Nothing will happen to enliven our faith unless we determine to do something about it. Circumstances may have caused the journey to become dry and dusty, but if we decide to act, the whole world of Christian faith is available to us – people to meet, places to go, courses to take, books to read, prayer to try. But there's no 'just add boiling water' solution to a flagging faith. We need to play fair with God and make some decisions for ourselves. Ultimately it's a choice. Do we want to re-embark on the ship of faith or wave a sad handkerchief as it departs? If we get on board, a whole world of new destinations, of fascinating encounters, of wonder and of mystery awaits us. And in God's graceful vessel everyone travels first class.

Story

At the start of a sabbatical I went on an eight-day Ignatian retreat. My guide for the week asked me how I was spiritually. I found I focused on two words: bland and compressed. 'Bland' meant that my spiritual experience was currently pretty ordinary, and 'compressed' meant that I felt restricted and under pressure in my work. My guide said that it would be good to start by not trying to do anything but simply to let God look at me with the gaze of accepting love. Gradually the pressure came off. I spent time each day with a passage of the Bible and drank in the richness of the encounter with God that lay underneath the words. I travelled through Psalm 139, Jesus' conversation with a Samaritan woman, the ministry of Jesus in Mark, Jesus' farewell teaching in John 15 and 16, the Passion in Mark and the resurrection in John. By the end of the eight days I had a fresh confidence in encountering Jesus in the Gospel stories, a renewed sense of the presence of God in all things, a desire to stay in the loving gaze of God, and a determination to attend to the experiences that speak of a larger world than my compressed one. It was a spiritual MOT and sent me off in good heart for the rest of the sabbatical.

Taking it further

When you have found the going sticky in your Christian journey, what has helped? Which of the ten ideas above would you commend to others and what other ones might you suggest?

15

Ten values for tomorrow's Church

It's strange that a Church that's been formed around a Man who died should be so afraid of death – institutional death, I mean. If churches are to be renewed, much of what has gone before will have to die. It's the way of nature; 50,000 cells in your body will have died and been replaced by new cells in the time it's taken you to read this sentence. Change is the way of institutions too, and we have to know when to let time-expired practices go. The Church of God has both a human and a divine nature. Referring to the latter, Rowan Williams described the Church as 'the community of those who have been immersed in Jesus' life, overwhelmed by it . . . who have disappeared under the surface of Christ's love and reappeared as different people'.[1] But the human, institutional life of this community has to be kept under constant review if it's to be a travelling company of spiritual seekers rather than a secret society of defensive administrators. And behind any organization is a set of values that determine its shape. What might these need to be for the journey ahead?

1 Inclusive welcome

> He drew a circle that shut me out,
> heretic, rebel, a thing to flout.
> But Love and I had the wit to win.
> We drew a circle that took him in.[2]

The Church at its best is a place where everyone is welcome, no one is perfect, and nothing is impossible. It needs to be a place where people at any stage on or off the spiritual journey can feel at home and know they'll be taken seriously, whether they're a devout believer or someone just tinged with faith – like those shades of white paint 'with a hint of peach'. The Church has to resist the temptation to become a gated community, exclusive and defensive. Tight boundaries of doctrine or ethics create sects, and the glory of the Church, following the unfailing practice of Jesus, is that it opens its doors to everyone, even (let it be known) Chelsea supporters, bankers, traffic wardens, and the odd jobbing bishop.

2 Energizing faith

Is this a value? Even if it isn't, it's a necessity. We have to be communities where a fire burns fiercely at the centre because that's where the passion comes from. People are drawn to a blazing fire where they won't turn their heads to a pile of ashes. What would be the point of being a church where faith in God was anaemic, perfunctory, downplayed, in case it upset the neighbours or the town council? Christians are sitting on a keg of dynamite, not running errands for the world. The most important task of church leadership, therefore, is to sustain the sacred centre of the Church's life and to draw people back, again and again, to the holy fire. You can recognize churches that have their 'central heating' in good working order because they're marked by justice and joy. Joy is the internal sign of the presence of Christ, and the pursuit of social justice is the external sign. Whatever else is working or not working in the life of the local church, this energizing faith is the key sign of life.

3 Christ-centred

The Church doesn't always cover itself with glory, but when it's being true to its calling, Jesus is always the main attraction. The famous words of Gandhi sum the situation up well: 'I like your

Christ; I do not like your Christians; your Christians are so unlike your Christ.'[3] But: 'I like your Christ.' The future Church mustn't be afraid of using its strongest suit and playing the Jesus card again and again. People will sometimes die for an ideology (usually a disastrous one), but they're much more likely to give their lives for a person. It's shining personalities like Nelson Mandela, Desmond Tutu or the Dalai Lama who attract people's wholehearted devotion. And none more than Jesus of Nazareth. This man was in the public eye for less time than it takes an undergraduate to get a degree, and yet he's inspired countless millions of people to change their lives and the lives of nations.

His values were flawless; his authority both secure and yet marked by humility; his judgement seemed to be spot on time after time; his teaching was radical and enthralling, his table-talk both challenging and entrancing. He was decisive, amusing, demanding and encouraging, and he filled his humanity to bursting point. But what was really different was that he left people strangely aware that they had been spending time with God. For my whole life as a Christian I've wanted to point people to this astonishing figure. I knew two sisters who were both in the Church Army, and at the age of 103 and 98 they moved to a new nursing home together. When they moved in, one of them said: 'Oh, good. A whole new mission field!' When Christ has taken hold of your life you never tire of telling others about him.

4 Engaged with the community

The writer G. K. Chesterton once wrote: 'A man [sic] can no more possess a private religion than he can have a private sun or moon.' Christian faith can't be a personal lifestyle accessory; it's about making a difference in the world. There's a tragic tendency for religious institutions to turn inwards and forget their original charism. Tom Wright suggests that they (as well as every Christian) go through a cycle of discovering God, loving God, institutionalizing God, domesticating God, and maybe even denying God, before, hopefully, discovering God again.[4] When faith is institutionalized and domesticated it has lost its way and got stuck in a corner. The faith we proclaim is unavoidably directed outwards. It propels us out into society to help align its life and values with those of the Kingdom of God, where the poor hear good news, the blind receive their sight and the oppressed go free (Luke 4.18). In a strange way this faith isn't for believers, it's for everyone else. The question a church should be asking is, 'How can we be a blessing to the community around us?'

Philip Pullman isn't a fan of organized religion, but he does see an ideal that many Christians would also own. In *The Poor Man Jesus and the Scoundrel Christ* he has Jesus praying to his Father in Gethsemane:

> that any church set up in your name should remain poor and powerless and modest. That it should wield no authority except that of love. That it should never cast anyone out. That it should own no property and make no laws. That it should not condemn but only forgive. That it should not be like a palace, with marble walls and polished floors, and guards standing at the door, but like a tree with its roots deep in the soil, that shelters every kind of bird and beast and gives blossom in the spring and shade in the hot sun and fruit in the season . . .

In an interview he went on: 'That's what I would like to see the church being like. Churches that serve the poor and pay no heed to the bullying of the rich. It does exist and I celebrate it.'[5] The Church at its best does indeed have its roots deep in local soil, there to serve the poor in the name of the one who had nowhere to lay his head. In future such engagement with the wider community will be non-negotiable if the local church is to survive. But if it does engage, the evidence is that it will grow.[6]

5 Participative and relational

Vibrant Christian communities are those that involve everyone in a web of loving, liberating relationships. They're graceful, relaxed, light-footed communities marked by warmth, encouragement, failure and forgiveness. They give people space to explore and experiment, to laugh at themselves, and to hibernate if necessary. They're places where you can raise questions, make mistakes, live differently and take risks. In such churches everyone matters. Children are consulted about what they want and their views are taken seriously. People with learning difficulties are received as if they too are Christ. Disagreements are handled sensitively and with grace. There's an emphasis on everybody growing in their faith and each stage of faith being respected and honoured. There's more interest in wisdom than efficiency, in following hunches rather than planning projects.

And where might these churches be? That's the problem. Such wonderful communities are as elusive as chocolate kettles. The difficulty is human nature. Nevertheless, these golden images give us a direction to pursue, and in the meantime there's much joy to be had on the journey. Pope John XXIII offered a pithy summary of what's needed in ecumenical relations which applies equally, I think, to local church life: 'In essentials, unity; in non-essentials, liberty; and in all things, charity.' And at the heart of a church that's trying to be faithful, there is, let us never forget, an inexhaustible source of life and inspiration – his Spirit is with us, bubbling up irrepressibly (John 4.14).

6 Whole-life discipleship

One of the hardest connections for a Christian to make is that between Sunday and Monday. On Sunday, faith can seem easy and life-giving. The link with home, family and leisure is clear. But on Monday the real-life decisions at work, over troubled family members, financial shortages or difficult neighbours, seem to be much less connected with the faith we celebrated on Sunday morning. There's an unreality about Sunday's somewhat bland encouragement to love our neighbour, to be honest and to pray. Come the evening and the television news is full of major problems and tough issues, and we find we don't have the equipment to face these questions from a Christian perspective, though we feel sure that we should. The problem is deep. Put simply, the one hour we spend in church doesn't prepare us well for the 167 other hours when we're in our 'normal' lives.

The Church of the future has got to address this disconnection, or Christians are going to become ever more vulnerable in a culture that presses us either to be wholehearted in our faith or to give up. We're going to need a robust, whole-life discipleship if we're to stand up to the secularizing pressures of the day. Churches, therefore, are going to have to start with real-life issues and bring the resources of the faith to bear on them, rather than inflating a bubble of church activities disconnected from the places where the shoe pinches in the hope that people will get by on a wave of shiny Christian goodwill. Sadly, Humpty-Dumpty has fallen off that wall time after time and all the King's pastors and all the King's clergy have not been able to put him back together again. On the other hand, a Christian living his or her faith in an informed, open, clear-eyed way, with integrity and wisdom, is a hugely attractive witness to the King and the King's priorities. Churches will have to resource that whole-life discipleship intentionally and robustly – or suffer the consequences.

7 Quality in worship

People are used to a high standard of communication, whether in films, television shows, work presentations, advertising promotions or charity campaigns. If churches then subject people to inadequately organized events in draughty, badly lit church halls with ancient, stuttering technology, the Lord is not being well served by his followers. This also applies to worship, the shop window of the faith. I'm impressed by the level of care that goes into preparing worship today. There's plenty of evidence of thoughtful preparation of services that are well signposted for regulars and visitors alike. Seasonal booklets and dedicated service sheets are matched by a variety of musical resources and careful attention to light and sound.

The problem we have lies further back. Are we still working on the assumption that what worked 20, or even ten, years ago will meet the needs of today's generation of churchgoers or 'might-be' churchgoers? Do we work on the principle that our worship might be a bit predictable (boring?) but ultimately it's good for you? Are we trying so much to 'carry everybody with us', or not offend anyone, that we're actually losing touch with what people want and need? Do we ask them? Does our worship need to be a bit more 'liquid' rather than 'heavy'? The imposs-ible but exciting task in designing worship is to be in touch with people's cultural presuppositions without dumbing down, to offer worship that's deep, varied and flexible, but remains true to the immense richness of the many traditions on which we can call. It starts with consulting the congregation, espe-cially the 'occasionals', and being rigorous in connecting their perceptions with the best liturgical thinking. It's a tall order, but that's the fun of it!

8 Joyful, playful and celebratory

Don't get me wrong – I don't want churches that are superficial and childish, and where serious exploration of the faith and the world we live in are banished in a welter of bouncy castles and family fun days. But we need to remember that Christians are not completely different from the rest of society and they too look for experiences that they'll enjoy, that will allow them to celebrate the goodness of God, and that will let them explore

what Jesus meant when he said that if we're to enter the Kingdom of God we'll have to become like a little child (Mark 10.15).
Our inner child is often told in church to behave and keep quiet
because this is serious business. Yes, but the most serious things
usually need the full panoply of human emotions to do them
justice. Churches are places where our humanity, in all its richness, should be given generous space and encouragement.

One wise bishop used to say that what he encouraged his
clergy to concentrate on was prayer and parties. When I talk
to friends about what they remember from the times we shared
in a parish in Taunton, they usually speak of the experiences
that touched both heights and depths in our community life.
There were hundreds of Sunday services that undoubtedly
watered the soul but it was the deep discoveries and the high
places that remain in the mind – the Passion play that brought
the town to a halt, living and fasting in a shack on the High
Street for Christian Aid, courses exploring silent prayer, starting
an adult education programme for the town, developing a
healing ministry that accompanied many people through dark
places; and also the parish camps, the Holy Land pilgrimages,
the mushrooming of children's work, the weeks in the Lake
District, the cricket matches, the Feasts. At its best, church is
an anticipation of heaven, and I take it that will involve much
celebration and joy – and almost certainly cricket.

9 Story-shaped

Just as that parish in Taunton was shaped by its stories, so the
whole Christian community is formed by the great story of
God's loving action in Jesus Christ. The devil may have the best
tunes but Christians have the best story. In a sceptical culture
the one thing we must keep doing is telling that story. People
may not be convinced by our theology or our worship but they
remain fascinated by the story when it's well told. And telling
that story is becoming more urgent as it's increasingly in danger

of slipping out of our cultural memory. The churches of our land need to tell that story in schools, in sermons and teaching, in DVDs, in drama and poetry, in art and music, and above all in describing how that great story has interacted with our own personal stories and shaped our lives. We live in a sea of stories; they pervade our media, our films, soaps, adverts, magazines, novels, conversations, text messages and tweets. Churches too are storytelling communities, where we share each other's lives and where together we allow ourselves to be shaped by the great narrative of Jesus. The Church needs to see itself as a community of storytellers, each person having his or her own angle on the story and their own style of telling it. It mustn't be The Greatest Story Never Told.

10 Depth

One quality our age most needs is depth. We live in a restless and rootless world where our hard-won reserves of wisdom and faith are rapidly being used up. New technologies give us access to everything all the time, and that often means that we skim over the surface of things, scooping up morsels of knowledge but not allowing ourselves the benefits of deep encounter. This is an exaggeration, of course, but it's worth pondering the dangers of a society that has access to so much information that people have to trivialize it to survive. Better to skim over it, we think, than to drown in it.

Church, therefore, needs to be one place where depth is not sacrificed to relevance. Thoughtful people look for a thoughtful faith and superficial answers won't do. The Franciscan writer Richard Rohr speaks of a 'first half of life culture' which is largely concerned with achievement and success. But, he says, it takes us much longer to discover 'the task within the task', what we're doing under the surface, and why.[7] Our Western minds are deeply dualistic (either–or), so we don't handle paradox very well, and yet life constantly throws up such paradoxes and we mustn't be afraid and run for cover when they confront us. We usually look for easy-fix answers to take away our pain when actually we need to learn to stay in the hard place and redeem it. David Runcorn wisely says: 'In the journey of the soul the Christian probably travels fastest by night.'[8] We grow much more when we've had to struggle than when life has been sweet and seamless.

Churches, then, will need to be places of realism, thoughtfulness, enquiry and doubt, as well as centres of deep spirituality. We mustn't peddle instant answers to hard questions; the pearl of great price may be stuck in the cracks of the pavement and need to be prised out very carefully. Sermons need to stimulate questions and suggest lines of enquiry. Clergy need to be mentors and coaches more than authoritative teachers. This is an age when the Wisdom tradition is coming into its own.

Story

A decaying monastery only had a few monks left. The abbot went to talk to a holy man about the tragedy and they spent many hours together. Finally, as the abbot was about to leave, the holy man suddenly said: 'There is, however, one thing you should know – the Messiah is among you.' The abbot puzzled over what these words meant, but he still told his brothers back at the monastery: 'It seems the Messiah is among us.'

The brothers got on with life but they pondered what those words meant. Was one of them the Messiah? Who could it possibly be? Could it even be me? They began to treat each other with new respect on the off-chance that one of them really might be the Messiah. They even began to treat themselves with new respect. When people came to the monastery they began to notice a powerful spiritual aura. Something was happening.

More visitors began to arrive. People brought their friends, who in turn brought their friends. Some of the younger people started to talk more and more with the older monks and after a while one of them asked if he could join the Order. Then another joined, and another. Within a few years the monastery was once again a thriving community. But they never discovered which of them was the Messiah.

————————

Taking it further

Which of the ten points above do you most agree with? What else would be in your list? How well does your own church embrace these values? What can you do to help your church become more like it needs to be for its future task?

16

Ten lessons learned

As we reach the end of this book, please excuse my self-indulgence. I want to reflect on rather a lot of years as a Christian and see what I've learned from them, in the hope that some of the lessons might be useful to others. I've chosen to attach these ruminations to the places that have been significant to my journey as a priest in the Church of England, but that's merely a device, a convenient way of locating what I was learning. Indulge me.

1 Commitment matters: university

I wonder how you would describe your relationship with God? Would you say you were strangers, acquaintances, dating, engaged, co-habiting, happily married, unhappily married, separated, divorced, or something else? For a long time God and I had been acquaintances – at least from my side; he'd always been committed to me, I later discovered. I'd skated around the Christian ice rink for many years but most of the experience seemed to be about enjoying my fellow skaters and avoiding falling over. I hadn't quite realized what it was all about. Specifically, I hadn't realized *who* it was all about. I hadn't taken in that the Master Skater was at the centre of things, trying to teach us to be champions. (I'd better leave this analogy before it gets out of control . . .)

There comes a time when a growing relationship comes to a tipping point. Is this it? Is this going to be my core partnership, because if it is, I need to get serious; it's the point of commitment. So with faith. Until that point, we're keeping our options open, looking from the outside in. Commitment is about looking from the inside out, and it makes all the difference in the world. This person (whether Christ or your loved one) is now your point of reference. From *within* this relationship you see everything else. It doesn't mean that you don't have any questions or that it isn't a struggle sometimes to adjust to the new commitment, but it does mean that this is now your vantage point. In terms of Christian commitment the journey that actually started quite a while ago (very few people come to commitment from nowhere) is now properly under way. It has fresh clarity, purpose and verve. God is a reality, not just an idea. There's energy in faith and hunger in prayer. The Christian life is full of possibility. I've long appreciated the words of a history professor from Cambridge who ended a book: 'Hold [fast] to Christ, and for the rest be totally uncommitted.'[1] If we get the heart of the faith right, everything else can be worked out from there. This crucial move happened for me while I was an undergraduate at Oxford.

2 Enthusiasm is not enough: Birmingham

I went to serve as a curate in the centre of Birmingham, bringing all my enthusiasm and idealism to the task after six years in the rarefied atmosphere of two universities. Surrounded by the needs and crises of a city centre – homelessness, addictions, loneliness, poverty, terrorist attacks – I was as energetic as a young pony (and probably about as useful). But in a newly unstructured life I failed at a basic level: I cut off the oxygen supply of faith, which is prayer. Not entirely, of course, but I promised God the best time of the day for prayer and then found that the best time of the day was very useful for all sorts of other things. It took me a while to realize what was happening.

A Christian life without prayer and attentiveness to God is going nowhere. The image Jesus uses is of being cut off from the vine. 'Abide in me, as I abide in you. Just as the branch cannot bear fruit by itself unless it abides in the vine, neither can you unless you abide in me' (John 15.4). No relationship between two people can flourish if they don't spend time together, discussing their thoughts, hopes, preoccupations and the everyday things that build up a shared life. Although it's a wee bit different when we're sharing with the God of Everything, the point about time spent together is the same. We give time to what matters to us and God matters supremely. I soon discovered, like the Israelites in the wilderness, that you can't keep manna in store; it comes fresh every day or not at all. Enthusiasm is not enough. We have to be rooted in Christ front and centre, first and last.

3 You can never be too 'apologetic': Wells

There's nothing like working with young people to sharpen up what you really believe. After enjoying a lot of youth work in Birmingham I went to be Diocesan Youth Officer in the diocese of Bath and Wells. Here I was meeting young people in schools, churches and youth clubs, and encountering the uncompromisingly direct questions they had about the Christian faith. Deference isn't a quality teenagers bother about very much and I was quickly having to brush up on what's called 'apologetics' – or how to defend and commend the Christian faith. It was exhilarating.

It's been said that the average British churchgoer is as well prepared to meet an aggressive atheist as a boy with a peashooter is to meet a tank. Key questions about the credibility of belief are flying around our culture even more than when I was a Youth Officer. Atheism is both respectable and vocal. How can you believe in God in an age of science? How can a loving God allow such appalling suffering? How can you believe that a carpenter from Nazareth was somehow God? When there are so many world religions why is Christianity special? And so on. These questions are alive and well *within* our churches as well as outside, and properly so. Churches need to find many ways of equipping today's

Christians to be more confident in answering such questions clearly and graciously, through sermons, courses, books, CDs and DVDs, signposting to internet sites, and so on. We need a growing confidence that faith isn't something intelligent adults grow out of, as so many assume, but rather faith is something we grow into, always deeper and wiser than we thought.

4 We learn by doing and failing: Taunton

I went to Taunton to be vicar of a parish. I was 31 with a young wife, two small children and a golden retriever, so I couldn't go wrong. But of course I did. A lot of things went well; we developed ministries in prayer, music and drama, in education, pastoral care and healing, in world development and evangelism. Our children's work began to fly and links with schools burgeoned. The church grew substantially. But unfortunately I sacked the choir. This was not a good move, and although it wasn't actually true, that's how it was reported. I also made a mess of some pastoral relationships that concern me still. I was insufficiently supportive of colleagues and I guess I drove forward my own agenda pretty single-mindedly. I had a lot to learn.

But that's how we *do* learn – by doing and sometimes failing. I owe so much to patient friends and colleagues in every role I've had as I've bustled in, messed up and learned something new. Learning is never finished. When my father was in his eighties he was still buying scholarly commentaries because he was a lifelong student. We've never fully learned what it is to be a Christian; there's always more. Mark Oakley said in a radio broadcast: 'God's gift to us is our being; our gift to God is our becoming.'[2] We always have more 'becoming' to do, if only because the goal is that we come 'to maturity, to the measure of the full stature of Christ' (Eph. 4.13). We all have a long way to go, and the beauty of it is that God will always turn out to be larger than we imagined. In the Narnia stories, Aslan the lion represents Jesus:

'Aslan,' said Lucy, 'you're bigger.'

'That is because you are older, little one,' answered he.

'Not because you are?'

'I am not. But every year you grow, you will find me bigger.'[3]

5 *Context is crucial: Durham*

Having been delighted with parish ministry I thought I might try and offer some of my enthusiasm to the next generation of clergy and so found myself in Durham, teaching at a theological college. It was here I finally twigged how important context is to the Church's mission. The North East is a wonderful region, lost for many people somewhere between Yorkshire and Scotland, but for those who find it, it's a marvel. It has some of the finest scenery in the country, the best castles and a panoply of inspiring saints, together with the friendliest people and the proudest and most tragic industrial past. Iron and steel has gone, the coal mines have all closed, shipbuilding has disappeared, even call centres have gone to India. And yet these brave, resilient north-easterners pick themselves up and carry on, even if their voices sound very muted to those making decisions in London. Cranmer Hall prided itself on taking its north-eastern context seriously and every student had to do some work at our Urban Mission Centre in Gateshead. Our placements often gave students their richest learning experience.

I realized then that Christians have to take the world as seriously as God takes it. We have to understand what's going on around us economically, politically, socially and culturally. We have to understand the issues and the passions (easy in the North East – football) and do all we can to reflect Christianly (theologically) on our context, because that's where God has placed us and that's where we have to live and interpret our faith. What is God doing in the North East? What's the Good News for the North East? What does God need his people to do here? The faith itself is gloriously given to us, handed down in unbroken form, but it works out differently for Christians in northern Nigeria, New York, India or Russia. Context is crucial.

6 Tell it slant: Canterbury

I moved on to Canterbury to be the Archdeacon and a residentiary canon of that sublime cathedral. It was a huge privilege to serve a place that meant so much to millions of Christians all over the world and I fell in love with it. I witnessed the multitude of roles it has to play – primarily a house of prayer and pilgrimage, but also a setting for great music, the making of films, the staging of plays (*Murder in the Cathedral* being an obvious one), for art exhibitions and lectures, for poetry and children's events. I began to realize how much people respond to God and the beauty of faith through the arts. I wasn't completely unaware of this, of course, but it struck me forcibly that 'telling it slant' (poet Emily Dickinson's phrase) is a deeply significant way of introducing and deepening faith.

The Christian faith has been responsible for some of the most memorable music, art, architecture, poetry and literature of the last 2,000 years. These things move many people more than they might want to admit. One of the tasks of the Church is to re-enchant a culture that has often become utilitarian and prosaic, and we have at our side an extraordinary treasure store on which to draw. In a sense, we have to set the world dreaming again and the arts can take people to the doorway of that enchanted world of faith. Whether they walk through the door is a personal decision based on many factors, but at least they may have caught a glimpse of a larger world.

7 Life's a building site: Jarrow

After five years in Canterbury we moved back to the North East, where I was to be Bishop of Jarrow. It was a happy return for us and I set about understanding what was required of a bishop in such a fascinating place. What I found, of course, was a complex picture and a vast number of loose ends. Nothing was clear cut; there were no straightforward solutions; nothing ever seemed to be finished. In other words, life was messy. It was always a building site. In terms that some will be familiar with I am a 'completer-finisher', so this messy dimension of church and community life was frustrating.

What it confirmed for me, however, is that it's entirely predictable that ministry should be messy because so is everything – politics, social progress, family life, my own life. Why should church life be any different? God's evolutionary method is itself incredibly messy but it provides the framework for everything we value – freedom, love, courage, discovery. Dare we say that God loves mess rather than everything boxed, labelled and tidy? Christians get discouraged by the messiness of the Church and we shouldn't be complacent about our sinfulness, but it couldn't be any other way in a world like ours. The Church needs to be loved and valued in its tangible reality, in part also because there's always another dimension to the Church, not easily accessible to the eye. Rowan Williams puts it like this:

> There is a lot to be said for understanding the Church itself as bigger on the inside than on the outside, with all that might mean for the priorities of Christian life: what matters most is not necessarily the figure that the Church cuts in the world but what is transformingly going on in the shared life of its members – which won't lend itself much to sound bites or dramatic images a lot of the time.[4]

Life may be a building site, but the Kingdom takes time.

8 Do your best, then let it go: Oxford

Presumably because of a shortage of candidates, I was then asked to be Bishop of Oxford. I knew that it would take all I'd ever learned and more. True to form, I often find I'm out of my depth and struggling to stay afloat. But at least I know that I'm trying to be the best that I can be and, knowing that, I can let go of attempting to achieve what's beyond me and trust in the goodness of God. It's like floating in grace.

When we're younger we're understandably filled with zeal to achieve all we can as soon as we can. So much is possible. As we begin to achieve those targets perhaps we find our goals changing. Living with integrity is more important than success in everything. Rich relationships are more important than an unnecessarily large bank balance (never a risk in my case). A broad enjoyment of life's gifts is more important than a narrow focus on the next step up the ladder. In fact, I only ever wanted to be a vicar but life has given me other opportunities and I took each of them with gratitude but always with trepidation. How good to reach the point where we can say that we have done our best and can therefore let it go, trustingly, into the hands of God.

9 Here is the best place: everywhere

I know I've been fortunate. I've loved every role I've had. That clearly isn't the case for every Christian, whether involved in public ministry or not. Some jobs are a struggle, with incessant problems and few rewards. But at some level I still want to maintain that here is the best place to be because here is the only place we can meet God. Jesuits teach persistently that God is in all things, not *causing* them necessarily, but *available* in them, ready to help, teach and redeem. It's obvious really; we can't meet God in the past (which is memory) or in the future (which is hope), but only in the present, where all of God is available to all of ourselves that we give him. Hankering after a golden past or an elusive future won't change the present; only God's ample presence can do that. 'Today, if you hear his voice, do not harden your hearts' (Heb. 4.7), because God's rest, his capacious *shalom*, is always available here, now, 'today'.

10 God is good – elusive, but good: everywhere

There's a refrain I picked up along the way that says: 'God is good, all of the time. All of the time, God is good.' Of course, many would have reason to doubt that confidence. Life has been tough for them and God has either been absent or unhelpful. But that simple affirmation of God's goodness isn't a trivial soundbite; it's a theological statement of real importance. The New Testament is unequivocal in teaching that God is love, that he is as he is seen in Jesus, and that he is to be trusted. When speaking of God we risk absurdity, toddlers playing at university, but when we've used up all our efforts trying to sift the complexity of a Mystery we can never contain, we're left with a single gold nugget: that God is good – always and everywhere. If we abandon that primary conviction, chaos is let loose. Not that we hold on to the conviction for fear of that consequence; it's simply to emphasize how basic the assertion is. 'God is light, and in him there is no darkness at all' (1 John 1.5). God will always be elusive – how could it be otherwise? – but he is always good. On that I stake my life.

Taking it further

Removing the personal story of the above as unnecessary context, do those ten lessons make sense to you? What would be your 'life lessons'? Can our life lessons be truly helpful to other people, or are they necessarily unique and therefore of limited use to others?

17

Ten reasons to procrastinate about faith

1

Notes

1 Ten problems people have with faith

1 Rabbi Jonathan Sacks, lecture in the series *Judaism and Modernity*, October 2011.
2 Richard Dawkins, *The God Delusion* (London: Bantam Press, 2006), p. 31.
3 Julian Baggini, *The Independent*, 4 September 2010.
4 John Polkinghorne, interview for *York Courses*, 2012.
5 Max Planck, read recently and lost – but widely available on the internet.
6 Albert Einstein, *Letter to Eric Gutkind*, 3 January 1954.
7 David Bentley Hart, *Atheist Delusions* (New Haven, CT: Yale University Press, 2009), p. 13.
8 Algernon Swinburne, *Hymn to Proserpine.*
9 Marilynne Robinson, interview in *Church Times*, 22 June 2012.
10 Charles Clarke, *The Tablet*, 28 January 2012.
11 Jeremy O'Grady, *The Week*, 19 May 2012.

2 Ten things I believe about God

1 John V. Taylor; see chapters 7 and 8 of *The Christlike God* (London: SCM Press, 1992) for a full exploration.
2 John V. Taylor, *A Matter of Life and Death* (London: SCM Press, 1986), p. 18.
3 The quote is from Michael Ramsey but often also associated with John V. Taylor.
4 Chris Russell, *To Be Delivered in the Event of My Death: Ten Letters* (London: Darton, Longman and Todd, 2012), p. 166.
5 C. S. Lewis, *The Lion, the Witch and the Wardrobe* (various editions), chapter 8.

3 Ten things I don't believe about God

1 Peter Tatchell, *New Statesman*, 4 February 2008.
2 Jamie Whyte, article in *The Guardian*, date untraced.
3 Julian Baggini, *The Independent*, 4 September 2010.
4 Terry Eagleton, *The Guardian*, 14 January 2012.
5 Richard Rohr, *Falling Upward* (London: SPCK, 2012), p. 106.
6 Rabbi Hugo Gryn, *Chasing Shadows* (London: Penguin, 2000), p. 250.

5 Ten reasons to believe in God

1 For a full discussion of the distinction between different kinds of knowledge see Iain McGilchrist, *The Master and his Emissary: The Divided Brain and the Making of the Western World* (New Haven, CT: Yale University Press, 2nd edn, 2012).
2 St Bonaventure, *The Soul's Journey into God*, in *Bonaventure* (New York: Paulist Press, 1978), p. 101.
3 Rowan Williams, *The Times*, 22 April 2011.
4 Rowan Williams, explored in chapter 3 of *Tokens of Trust* (Norwich: Canterbury Press, 2007).
5 Francis Spufford, *Unapologetic: Why Despite Everything Christianity Can Still Make Surprising Emotional Sense* (London: Faber and Faber, 2012), p. 19.
6 Yann Martel, *Life of Pi* (London: Canongate Books, 2003).

6 Ten beliefs about science and religion

1 Karl Gilbertson and Francis Collins, *The Language of Science and Faith* (London: SPCK, 2011), p. 86.
2 John Polkinghorne, *Science and Religion in Quest of Truth* (London: SPCK, 2011), p. 29.
3 Timothy Radcliffe, *The Tablet*, 7 May 2005.
4 Jonathan Sacks, *The Great Partnership* (London: Hodder and Stoughton, 2011).
5 Gilbertson and Collins, *The Language of Science and Faith*, p. 83.
6 John Polkinghorne, *Resource magazine*, Summer 2012.

7 John Polkinghorne and Nicholas Beale, *Questions of Truth* (Louisville, KY: Westminster John Knox Press, 2009), p. 37.

7 Ten Bible passages that tell the whole story

1 Robert Farrar Capon, *The Third Peacock* (San Francisco: Harper and Row, 1986), p. 9.
2 G. K. Chesterton, *What's Wrong with the World* (1910), ch. 5.
3 David Bentley Hart, *Atheist Delusions* (New Haven, CT: Yale University Press, 2009), p. 11.
4 St John Chrysostom, from the sermon *On Lazarus*.

8 Ten key beliefs about Jesus

1 Rowan Williams, *Tokens of Trust* (Norwich: Canterbury Press, 2007), p. 76.
2 A model developed in Williams, *Tokens of Trust*, p. 72.
3 Albert Einstein, various sources, widely available on the internet.
4 Alison Morgan, *The Wild Gospel* (Oxford: Monarch, 2004), p. 234.
5 N. T. Wright, *The Resurrection of the Son of God* (London: SPCK, 2003).
6 David Ford, *The Shape of Living* (Grand Rapids, MI: Baker, 1997).
7 Chris Russell, *To Be Delivered in the Event of My Death: Ten Letters* (London: Darton, Longman and Todd, 2012), p. 16.
8 John McCarthy and Jill Morrell, *Some Other Rainbow* (London: Bantam Press, 1993).
9 Bono, quoted in Tim Keller, *The Reason for God* (London: Hodder and Stoughton, 2009), p. 229.

9 Ten reasons why Christianity is so long lasting

1 Simone Weil, *Goodreads* website.
2 *Sunday Times Magazine*, 2 January 2011.
3 Words on a piece of paper smuggled out of Bonhoeffer's cell shortly before he was hanged at Flossenbürg in 1945.
4 A tale told by James Martin SJ in his book *The Jesuit Guide to Almost Everything* (New York: HarperOne, 2010), p. 211.

10 Ten Commandments for today

1 Letter in *The Guardian*, reprinted in *The Week*, 12 January 2013.
2 BBC One, 24 September 2011.

11 Ten clichés to avoid

1 *Church Times*, 3 and 10 August 2012.
2 Quoted by Martyn Percy in *Reflections for Daily Prayer* (London: Church House Publishing, 2012), p. 66.

13 Ten sustaining prayers

1 *An Anglican Prayer Book* (Church of the Province of Southern Africa, 1989).
2 Bishop Peter Nott: used with permission.
3 This copyright material is taken from *A New Zealand Prayer Book – He Karakia Mihinare o Aotearoa* (Christchurch: Genesis Publications, 1989). It is used with permission.
4 David Adam, *The Edge of Glory* (London: Triangle/SPCK, 1985), p. 76.
5 *A New Zealand Prayer Book.*

14 Ten ways to enliven your faith

1 Brother Lawrence, *The Practice of the Presence of God*, numerous editions.
2 Source untraced, but widely available on the internet.
3 Tom Wright, *Mark for Everyone* (London: SPCK, 2001).

15 Ten values for tomorrow's Church

1 Rowan Williams, *Tokens of Trust* (Norwich: Canterbury Press, 2007), p. 112.
2 Edward Markham, 'Outwitted', from *The Shoes of Happiness and Other Poems* (1913).
3 Mahatma Gandhi, source untraced but widely available on the internet.

4 Tom Wright, *The Way of the Lord* (London: SPCK, 1999), p. 65.

5 Philip Pullman, article in magazine *Reform*, October 2010.

6 Church Urban Fund, *Growing Church through Social Action*, February 2012.

7 Richard Rohr, *Falling Upward* (London: SPCK, 2012), p. xiv.

8 David Runcorn, *The Road to Growth Less Travelled* (Cambridge: Grove Publishing, 2008).

16 Ten lessons learned

1 Herbert Butterfield, *Christianity and History* (London: Fontana, 1957), p. 189.

2 In the Sunday Service, BBC Radio 4, 3 February 2013.

3 C. S. Lewis, *Prince Caspian* (London: HarperCollins, 2010), p. 380.

4 Rowan Williams, *The Lion's World* (London: SPCK, 2012), p. 134.

Printed and bound by CPI Group (UK) Ltd, Croydon, CR0 4YY

25/03/2025

14647340-0005